GUIDE

Vol 42 / Part 2
May 2026

Edited by **Rachel Tranter and Olivia Warburton**

7	**Ecclesiastes** M. J. Kramer	*4–10 May*
15	**1 and 2 Timothy** Stephanie Addenbrooke Bean	*11–24 May*
30	**Isaiah of Jerusalem** Henry Wansbrough	*25 May–7 June*
45	**Theology of mental health** Rachael Newham	*8–14 June*
54	**Malachi: the six disputes** Olivia Warburton	*15–21 June*
62	**Grace in the New Testament** David Spriggs	*22 June–5 July*
77	**2 Samuel 11—24: David the king: failure and fallout** Walter Moberly	*6–19 July*
92	**Matthew: forgiveness and reconciliation** Tim Welch	*20 July–2 August*
107	**Ezra** Miriam Bier Hinksman	*3–16 August*
122	**Job 1—13: A geography of suffering** Tanya Marlow	*17–30 August*

BRF Ministries
15 The Chambers, Vineyard
Abingdon OX14 3FE
brf.org.uk | 01865 319700

Bible Reading Fellowship is a charity (233280) and company limited by guarantee (301324), registered in England and Wales

EU Authorised Representative: Easy Access System Europe – Mustamäe tee 50, 10621 Tallinn, Estonia, **gpsr.requests@easproject.com**

ISBN 978 1 80039 482 7

Distributed in Australia by:
MediaCom Education Inc, PO Box 610, Unley, SA 5061
Tel: 1 800 811 311 | admin@mediacom.org.au

Distributed in New Zealand by:
Scripture Union Wholesale, PO Box 760, Wellington
Tel: 04 385 0421 | suwholesale@clear.net.nz

Acknowledgements
Scripture quotations marked with the following abbreviations are taken from the version shown. Where no abbreviation is given, the quotation is taken from the version stated in the contributor's introduction.

A catalogue record for this book is available from the British Library

Printed and bound in the UK by Zenith Media NP4 0DQ

Suggestions for using *Guidelines*

Set aside a regular time and place, if possible, when and where you can read and pray undisturbed. Before you begin, take time to be still and, if you find it helpful, use the BRF Ministries prayer on page 6.

In *Guidelines*, the introductory section provides context for the passages or themes to be studied, while the units of comment can be used daily, weekly or whatever best fits your timetable. You will need a Bible (more than one if you want to compare different translations) as Bible passages are not included. Please don't be tempted to skip the Bible reading because you know the passage well. We will have utterly failed if we don't bring our readers into engagement with the word of God. At the end of each week is a 'Guidelines' section, offering further thoughts about, or practical application of, what you have been studying.

Occasionally, you may read something in *Guidelines* that you find particularly challenging, even uncomfortable. This is inevitable in a series of notes which draws on a wide spectrum of contributors and doesn't believe in ducking difficult issues. Indeed, we believe that *Guidelines* readers much prefer thought-provoking material to a bland diet that only confirms what they already think.

If you do disagree with a contributor, you may find it helpful to go through these three steps. First, think about why you feel uncomfortable. Perhaps this is an idea that is new to you, or you are not happy about the way something has been expressed. Or there may be something more substantial – you may feel that the writer is guilty of sweeping generalisation, factual error, or theological or ethical misjudgement. Second, pray that God would use this disagreement to teach you more about his word and about yourself. Third, have a deeper read about the issue. There are further reading suggestions at the end of each writer's block of notes. And then, do feel free to write to the contributor or the editor of *Guidelines*. We welcome communication, by email, phone or letter, as it enables us to discover what has been useful, challenging or infuriating for our readers. We don't always promise to change things, but we will always listen and think about your ideas, complaints or suggestions. Thank you!

To send feedback, please email **enquiries@brf.org.uk**, phone **+44 (0)1865 319700** or write to the address shown opposite.

Writers in this issue

M. J. Kramer is chaplain of Keble College, Oxford, having previously served as precentor of Canterbury Cathedral. His academic interests include classics, biblical studies and Hellenistic Judaism. He is also author of *The Canterbury Book of New Parish Prayers*.

Stephanie Addenbrooke Bean is a graduate of Yale University (BA) and Yale Divinity School (MDiv). She was a finalist in the 2022 Theology Slam and writes regularly on Substack (stephanieabean.substack.com).

Henry Wansbrough is a monk of Ampleforth, Yorkshire. He has been chairman of the Oxford Faculty of Theology and has also served on the Pope's Biblical Commission and on the Anglican Roman Catholic International Commission.

Rachael Newham is a freelance author and speaker specialising in the theology of mental health. She's worked with a number of Christian mental health charities. Her most recent book is *Beloved Is Where We Begin*. Her social media is @RachaelNewham90.

Olivia Warburton is co-editor of *Guidelines*. Formerly head of content creation and Living Faith ministry lead for BRF Ministries, she has worked in a number of editorial roles.

David Spriggs has been a Baptist minister for over 50 years. As well as national roles with the Evangelical Alliance and Bible Society, he has worked in six local churches, written a number of books and has a wife, three children and ten grandchildren.

Walter Moberly is Emeritus Professor of Theology and Biblical Interpretation at Durham University. He has recently written *Old Testament Theology*, *The Bible in a Disenchanted Age* and *The God of the Old Testament* (Baker Academic).

Tim Welch is lead chaplain at Cheltenham and Gloucester YMCA, and research fellow at Bristol Baptist College where he previously served as Director of Ministerial Formation. Tim is married to Rachel, and they live in Cheltenham.

Miriam Bier Hinksman is an Anglican priest in the diocese of Canterbury, as well as a biblical scholar, teacher, preacher, and writer. Her most recent work is *Reading Hosea: A beginner's guide* (Grove, 2023).

Tanya Marlow is a writer, speaker and lecturer who specialises in biblical narrative and honest theologies of disability and suffering. Her books include *Those Who Wait*, and you can download her first book for free at **TanyaMarlow.com**.

The editors write...

Olivia writes:

I've loved being *Guidelines* editor alongside Rachel for the past four years – where did the time go? – and I celebrate every issue that has been published in that time; every contributor who has explored and explained God's word for us. New full-time working commitments mean that I no longer have adequate time available to nurture and develop *Guidelines* in the way it deserves, but I am leaving it in Rachel's capable hands to take forward.

I want to say a heartfelt thankyou to all our readers for your partnership with us; for your invariably helpful, encouraging and challenging feedback; and above all for your desire for *Guidelines* to be a place of encounter with God. I wish you every blessing as you continue to ask, seek and receive.

Rachel writes:

Olivia and I have been editing *Guidelines* together since 2021. She has brought so much enthusiasm, wisdom, clear-headedness and encouragement to *Guidelines*, and I can't thank her enough for all of her contributions. It's a daunting task to continue to commission and edit by myself, but we have a superb group of contributors who make it very easy to take joy in the whole process.

For this issue, I'm delighted to introduce Rachael Newham, who writes movingly and frankly about a theology of mental health. It's also a pleasure to welcome back Henry Wansbrough, who last wrote in 2023. We have a host of other contributors for this issue, all of whom write brilliantly on their chosen topic. It is fitting, too, that Olivia leaves us with her wise and sensitive thoughts on Malachi as we celebrate her final issue with us.

Times of endings are always, inevitably, times of new beginnings as well. As we thank Olivia for her time working on *Guidelines*, we also look with expectation, joy and thankfulness to the future, and all that God will say in this new season.

With every blessing,

Rachel Olivia

The prayer of BRF Ministries

Faithful God,
thank you for growing BRF Ministries
from small beginnings
into the worldwide family it is today.
We rejoice as young and old
discover you through your word
and grow daily in faith and love.
Keep us humble in your service,
ambitious for your glory
and open to new opportunities.
For your name's sake.
Amen.

Helping to pay it forward

As part of our BRF Resources ministry, we're raising funds to give away copies of Bible reading notes and other resources to those who aren't able to access them any other way, working with food banks and chaplaincy services, in prisons, hospitals and care homes.

'This very generous gift will be hugely appreciated, and truly bless each recipient… Bless you for your kindness.'

'We would like to send our enormous thanks to all involved. Your generosity will have a significant impact and will help us to continue to provide support to local people in crisis, and for this we cannot thank you enough.'

If you've enjoyed and benefited from our resources, would you consider paying it forward to enable others to do so too?

Make a gift at **brf.org.uk/donate**

Ecclesiastes

M. J. Kramer

'Vanity of vanities, says the Teacher... All is vanity' (Ecclesiastes 1:2). The difficulty of interpreting Ecclesiastes is reflected in the fact that even the book's famous slogan is almost impossible to translate definitively. The word traditionally rendered 'vanity' (*hebel*) derives from a root meaning 'vapour/breath', but in virtually every case it has a more metaphorical meaning and can describe nothingness, futility, senselessness, transitoriness, emptiness and absurdity. What's more, the exact connotations of the term seem to vary across its multiple uses in the short text of Ecclesiastes. Perhaps this is only too appropriate for a word whose origins lie with a force – vapour, breath – that cannot be clearly seen or pinned down, an original physical meaning Ecclesiastes keeps active by repeatedly pairing *hebel* with the expression 'chasing after wind'.

This vapour-like, breathy elusiveness of Ecclesiastes' writing has often been a source of frustration to the book's readers, who seek to know what exactly its provocative author believes about God and human life. This frustration has led commentators to attempt to reconstruct a constructive argument from Ecclesiastes' more meandering form of expression, where each proposition emerges only to be dissolved into vapour, as it is replaced by another that often contradicts the first.

In these reflections, I want to suggest that we can get more out of this fascinating book by allowing ourselves to be blown around by the changing directions of Ecclesiastes' windy writing, rather than by trying to penetrate through it to uncover the stable convictions of a putative more systematic thinker. If we allow ourselves to do that, we will find ourselves emerging from our encounter with this book with a vision of human life that is more richly complicated – less clearly understood, perhaps, but also more fully explored.

Bible quotations are taken from the NRSV.

1 What's the point?

Ecclesiastes 1

To understand Ecclesiastes, we need to start halfway through the book's first chapter, after the opening poem has finished. In verses 12–18, we find a deliberate accumulation of first-person Hebrew verbs: 'I applied… I saw… I said… I applied… I perceived.' These remind us, as the character of the Teacher begins to speak in his own voice, that his objective is to draw us into his own particular perspective, his own stream of consciousness.

This can create a problem. Many of us are so accustomed to expect every Bible text to deliver a 'message' that we want to jump ahead, understand the Teacher's point and apply it to our lives today. But be warned! Those who try to do that with Ecclesiastes either find themselves tangled up in this text's contradictions or just prioritising the verses that accord with their preferred beliefs and ignoring the others.

The starting point of understanding Ecclesiastes is proclaimed in all those 'I's. The purpose of this book is not necessarily to present an objective message, but to give us a flavour of a particular subjective thought process. So perhaps it's better to approach Ecclesiastes less as a work of theology – addressing the question of 'how things *are*' – and more as a work of spirituality – 'how things *feel*'.

The subjectivity of the Teacher's 'take' on life can be seen at work in the opening poem (vv. 4–11). The succession of one generation to another and the reliable circularity of nature, to other eyes, might be a source of reassurance or even of wonder. Yet to the Teacher it is a source of tedium and pointlessness. There is 'nothing new under the sun' (v. 9), a point reinforced by the laboriously repeated Hebrew word-roots *hlk* (go) and *sbb* (return), which together make up around half of the words in verse 6.

For those of us tempted towards prioritising the stable and impersonal abstractions of doctrine, Ecclesiastes 1 reminds us that true theology is always embodied, and so – like the wind and the sun and the streams and the generations – it is always on the move, ebbing and flowing, because that movement is the nature of life. That is the nature of breath (*ruah*, *hebel*).

2 Experiments with hedonism

Ecclesiastes 2

Most of us want to be happy, and there is much in the Teacher's test of pleasure (v. 1) that sounds familiar. Not only has the Teacher tried the traditional youthful expedients of sex (v. 8c), drugs (v. 3), and rock and roll (v. 8b), but he has also experimented with rather more middle-aged pleasures: home-ownership (v. 4), gardening (vv. 5–6) and even a walk in the park (v. 5). Try as he might, however – try as we might – none of these really bring satisfaction. So the Teacher's lament that sometimes it just feels like a lot of wasted effort (v. 11) might sound all too familiar as well.

Now, it might be tempting here to leap in with a conventional conclusion, and perhaps Ecclesiastes is trying to encourage us to do so. *I get it – all the pleasures of life are empty. What we need to do is focus on God!* But if we give into that temptation, we are soon going to get a nasty surprise. Verses 13–14a at first sound very conventional. Indeed, the idea that wisdom trumps all the pleasures that we heard about in verses 1–11 would not have sounded out of place in the book of Proverbs.

It is what comes next that is the kicker. Wisdom exceeds folly as light exceeds darkness… but ultimately the same fate of death awaits fool and wise man alike. In the end, wisdom is no more the answer than wealth, or status, or alcohol – a seriously subversive statement indeed, especially when we remember that Ecclesiastes 1:1 identifies the Teacher as King Solomon, a man who was famously praised by God for praying for wisdom to discern what is right instead of 'long life or riches, or for the life of [his] enemies' (1 Kings 3:11).

In the end, it seems, there is no answer. The only consolation is to snatch what pleasure you can in food and drink and work (v. 24), before that too is taken from you.

The nihilistic outlook of this chapter might seem unappealing. Yet it is good to be reminded that our moments of despair do find a home within the biblical text itself. What's more, the failure of the Teacher's experiment, with its insistent 'I made… for myself' repetitions, reminds us that sometimes we have to accept that we can't always manufacture or force our own happiness.

In the end, perhaps there's more to life than being happy.

3 The great contradiction

Ecclesiastes 3

The opening verses of Ecclesiastes 3 are some of the most famous, and perhaps some of the most beautiful, in the Bible, with their lilting rhythm and their soothing, balanced repetitions. As they are often read at funerals, they have helped countless people to come to terms with the fact that sorrow, mourning and death are as much a part of our existence as joy, laughter and life.

Yet these lines are not the totality of chapter 3. Indeed, they are only really its introduction. For the nub of Ecclesiastes' thinking in this chapter comes in verse 11. '[God] has made everything suitable for its time; moreover [an emphatic *gam* in Hebrew] he has put [*'olam*] into their minds, yet they cannot find out what God has done from beginning to the end.' The Hebrew *'olam* is hard to translate. Often meaning world/everything/eternity, the NRSV paraphrases the word accurately for this context to mean 'a sense of past and future.'

In other words, human existence is in a constant state of tension. In one sense, as we live them out each day, our lives are cyclical, seasonal, repetitive, and this is something in which we can find refuge and, perhaps, consolation. Yet, in another sense, we have a need implanted deep within us to make sense of the *'olam*, the whole, the past and the future, a quest which the Teacher believes often leads us to desolation, and which is nonetheless inevitable.

When giving guidance to people who are struggling, I often encourage them to make sure they balance *coping* with *thinking about things*, advising them to make a space for grief or questioning, but also a space for doing the activities that can give them a break from all that. For Ecclesiastes, however, these two dimensions of life are active not only in the difficult times, but always. Humans must live with the contradictions of embracing our temporality while also engaging with our longing to understand the whole, eternal story.

Ecclesiastes 3, then, demonstrates the complexity but also the profundity of the Teacher's understanding of the human condition. To be human, for Ecclesiastes, is to experience the paradoxes of a life which is at once cyclical and linear, consoling and desolating, momentary and integral, fleshly and intellectual, knowing that, in the end, this wonderful bundle of paradoxes will unravel into the simplicities of earth, and breath, and dust.

4 What are we really looking for?

Ecclesiastes 4:1—5:7

Why do we go out to work in the morning? Most of us would usually respond to that question: to pay the bills, or, if we're lucky, because I love my job. But for the writer of Ecclesiastes, who is always keen to probe into the darker and more repressed corners of the human heart, the reality is that all work, all toil and all skill ultimately comes from a place of envy (4:4). What drives us to labour and to earn is a jealous desire of what others possess and the competitive instinct to have the same or, even better, more – stuff, status or leisure – than them.

We might not like that reflection, but if you are reading this, it's likely that you do indeed have more income than is required for basic subsistence, and Ecclesiastes might productively lead you honestly to ask yourself the question: why?

One result of Ecclesiastes' musings on work is something like the modern concept of the work–life balance (v. 6), but more interesting is his application of this ethic of resisting over-busyness to our relationship with God.

The first seven verses of chapter 5 are the only really extended treatment of the relationship of humanity to God in Ecclesiastes. So some readers tend to latch on to these verses to reclaim this problematic author for orthodoxy, by arguing that this passage, structurally 'central' in the text, shows that the solution to the emptiness of life is a conventional, obedient piety.

In reality, though, these verses have more the character of a warning than an exhortation to closer engagement with the divine. Indeed, in this pessimistic context, I'm inclined to read 5:5 quite literally: it is actually better not to get involved at all with holy vows, than to risk God's wrath for messing one up.

Read alongside the passage on toil, then, this cultic passage is equally provocative. What are we really looking for in a relationship with God? Have we turned our faith into another form of toil? Is our church-life becoming another form of busyness, or even rivalry? Perhaps sometimes we need simply to guard our steps and keep silence, and be reminded that the transcendent God is not something to be coopted as another instrument for our cultivation, manipulation and competitiveness.

5 Life in an uncertain universe

Ecclesiastes 7:1–25

Ecclesiastes 7 takes its reader on a disorientating intellectual journey. Its opening line seems reassuringly conventional at first: 'A good name is better than precious ointment.' Its apparent universal relevance is highlighted by an elegant play on words, as the Hebrew word for 'name' and 'ointment' are similar (*tob shem mi* and *shemen tob*). Finally, the reader might think, Ecclesiastes is returning to the familiar ethics of the wisdom tradition. Relax!

This conventional introduction, however, is only a tease. The immediate parallel to the opening conventional proverb is far more disturbing: the day of death is better than the day of birth. The sequence of maxims that follow mix the conventional (v. 5) with the topsy-turvy (v. 3), with dizzying effect. The reader who tries to keep up with this rapidly oscillating perspective is left more confused than enlightened – and perhaps this is precisely the point. As Seow (p. 246) puts it, 'the realities of life are simply too contradictory to be governed by axioms.' Perhaps the traditional wisdom project is doomed to fail.

What is even more provocative than this diagnosis of cosmic confusion is that Ecclesiastes advocates a revolutionary approach to life in this uncertain world (vv. 16–18). The 'Goldilocks' suggestion that we should aim to be neither be too good nor too wicked is a radical departure from the conventional religious morality that we should seek to be completely 'holy' (Leviticus 19:2) or 'perfect' (Matthew 5:48) and beg for divine forgiveness when we fail.

Theologically objectionable as it may be, however, there is something refreshingly honest about Ecclesiastes' realism that nobody is so righteous as never to sin (v. 20), and something potentially liberating about his suggestion that a degree of self-understanding, acceptance, and maybe even humour, might have a role to play in our response to our sins as well as the traditional exhortations to self-flagellation. Even if we are not willing to go so far, we might still see the value of a degree of reserve and provisionality about all our claims, actions and commitments in this complex world. Maybe acknowledging, rather than repressing, the compromises we make each day is a legitimate part of a holy – and healthy – life.

6 Dust to dust

Ecclesiastes 11—12

The contradictions of Ecclesiastes continue all the way through to the very end of the book. Indeed, in these final two chapters they intensify. We are to rejoice in the light of life, yet remember darkness and vanity (11:7–8); we are to rejoice in youth (11:9) and the good creation of God, but to remember the pains of old age (12:1–7); we are encouraged to banish anxiety from our minds (11:10), only to be told how much we have to be anxious about!

To the end, then, the text of Ecclesiastes maintains the ebb and flow of a work of spirituality, rather than settling down with the resolution of a work of doctrinal theology. Indeed, the text's love of paradox is not so different from the apparently contradictory descriptions of spiritual experience that echo throughout mystical literature – sober drunkenness, sweet pain, dazzling darkness – albeit, for Ecclesiastes, life's paradoxes are more intellectual than emotional in nature.

Ecclesiastes' final enigma, though, is expressed through a sophisticated manipulation of form. The explicit concern of the sentence that begins in 12:1 is the injunction to remember the creator in one's youth. The temporal subclause ('before…') however, is extended to such a degree that the original main clause is long forgotten in a heap of images that speak of old age and the end of life. In typically contradictory fashion, a verse that purports to encourage a focus on the moment of youth ends up tangled in a preoccupation with life's end, in a web of images whose expressive virtuosity and fecundity clashes with the dying away they purport to describe.

This highly poetic section forms an eloquent 'first ending' to the book. It leads not to a triumphant resolution, 'Q.E.D.', but rather a fizzling out in a string of disconnected images, fading to nothing, like a human life, melting away, into the chaotic dust and breath from which it first took on form.

A more definite final boundary is provided by 12:8–14. Often thought to 'correct' a sceptical thinker by imposing a more conventional, moralistic message, these verses can be read more functionally as drawing us out of the subjective consciousness of Ecclesiastes, to return us to our own everyday world. This is a return which leaves open the question of where the restless spirit that we have seen blow through this text might lead us next on our own spiritual journey.

Guidelines

If we read Ecclesiastes as a work of spirituality rather than theology, it seems right to conclude by considering how the book reflects your own spiritual and life experience. The book's complexity (not to say obscurity) has allowed its interpreters to combine its text with their own preoccupations, theologies and personal experiences, to produce a rich kaleidoscope of interpretations of this poetic masterpiece. These questions encourage you, like them, to bring your own self into dialogue with this ancient text.

Questions for reflection:

- How do your feelings about life compare to Ecclesiastes? Do you resonate with the tension between meaninglessness and enjoying simple pleasures?
- What do you do to 'make yourself happy' and does it work? When it doesn't, how do you cope?
- Does Ecclesiastes' suggestion not to be too righteous or too wicked make sense? Can it be reconciled with traditional Christian teaching, or your personal faith?
- What drives you to work, or to go on living, or to engage with God? Has reading Ecclesiastes changed your view about any of this?

FURTHER READING

Craig G. Bartholomew, *Ecclesiastes* (Baker Academic, 2014).
Peter Enns, *Ecclesiastes* (Eerdmans, 2011).
Michael V. Fox, *A Time to Tear Down and a Time to Build Up* (Wipf & Stock, 2010).
Arthur Jan Keefer, *Ecclesiastes and the Meaning of Life in the Ancient World* (CUP, 2022).
Tremper Longman III, *The Book of Ecclesiastes* (Eerdmans, 1998).
T. A. Perry, *The Book of Ecclesiastes (Qohelet) and the Path to Joyous Living* (CUP, 2015).
Choon-Leong Seow, *Ecclesiastes* (Yale UP, 2007).

1 and 2 Timothy

Stephanie Addenbrooke Bean

The two letters to Timothy from Paul are endearing messages of encouragement from a seasoned leader to a seemingly nervous one just beginning his ministry. But there are principles contained here for all of us, no matter our stage of faith or level of leadership. I have outlined in the subsequent notes Paul's guiding principles for a life of discipleship from these epistles, identifying twelve practices for solidifying our faith and witness to those around us.

Paul is particularly aware of false teachers and the damage they can do, and how easy it can be for them to infiltrate Christian communities. Scholars debate the identity of these external threats (as posed to Paul when he was writing), but it is not difficult for us to see the applicability of his message today.

As you read 1 and 2 Timothy over the next two weeks, I urge you to consider how you may heed Paul's advice so that you too can say in your final days that you 'fought the good fight' (2 Timothy 4:7) before resting with Christ in 'eternal glory' (2 Timothy 2:10).

Bible quotations are taken from the NIV.

1 Defending truth

1 Timothy 1:1–11

After pleasantries and introductions, Paul tells Timothy to stay in Ephesus. I used to be confused by this, presuming that Paul would want his 'best leaders' to continue his work of mission by travelling far and wide to spread the gospel. But as I have studied 1—2 Timothy more closely, I have been reminded of the usefulness of remaining in one place, particularly as it relates to combating false doctrine and defending truth. I have found that the most effective evangelism strategies come from building relationships and seeking to understand the place God has put us. Having one foot out of the door helps no one. Besides, if the true goal of teaching truth is love, as Paul indicates in verse 5, how can we develop such love if we are always seeking to move on? Perhaps defending the truth of the gospel is less about apologetics but instead about building loving relationships.

Paul writes that false doctrine is driven by selfish ambition more so than lack of understanding or being confused by scripture. This is an important distinction, but one that returns us to the importance of building relationships. False teachers seek popularity and fame. Confused individuals seek truth, even if they do not know yet how or where to find it. This should bring great comfort to those of us who are frequently befuddled by complex parts of scripture, but it should also give great impetus to those who teach the Bible. Defending truth requires knowing scripture so that it can be taught well and in line with apostolic teaching.

One of the confusing things about these first verses of 1 Timothy is the list of sins prohibited by Paul in verses 9 to 11. When we study them more carefully, though, we see that they are closely linked to those outlined in the Decalogue (Exodus 20:1–17). It is important to note this. Paul wants to distinguish that the law is not the route to salvation but that it remains useful. It is still the moral standard we must use. So, defending the truth of the gospel involves teaching the ten commandments and the other underlying principles found in the Old Testament law. If we teach these things in love and with the proper perspective, we're probably on the right track.

2 Recalling testimony

1 Timothy 1:12—2:7

When someone asks you why you're a Christian (presuming that you are), what do you say? I have had many answers over the years, but one thing is constant in my responses. To use the words of Paul in verse 14: 'the grace of our Lord was poured out on me abundantly.' And as Paul points to his former violent and blasphemous ways as a means to propel forward his argument that Christ died for everyone, so too can I do the same. Paul calls himself 'the worst' of sinners (v. 15). For me to do the same could be perceived as hyperbolic gesturing, but I think it is common to believe that if people really knew the truth about us, we wouldn't be liked as much, and we certainly wouldn't be worth dying for.

It's part of the reason why I find Paul an appealing and somewhat relatable figure in scripture. When I look at his prolific ministry, it is difficult to make that association. But, when I hear that he too struggled with his past, I am comforted. We all have things in our past (and sometimes our present too) which mean it's not hard to convince us that we have 'fall[en] short of the glory of God' (Romans 3:23). But instead of wallowing in self-pity and a failure to forgive himself, which is often my tendency, Paul recalls his former ways as a testimony to his current state. He proudly bears his testimony – as difficult as it may be – to demonstrate the grace and mercy of Christ.

In the verses that follow, Paul instructs Timothy to recall the prophecies spoken about him. It is wonderful to remember the grace and mercy bestowed upon us in our darkest moments. But it is also important to remember that we have each been uniquely called to something. Not all of us will have heard clear prophetic words, as Timothy seemingly did, but each of us was lovingly created for a purpose. We each have been given gifts and qualities that reveal the goodness of God here on earth. So while we are certainly sinners saved by grace, to 'fight the battle well' (v. 18) we need to focus on who we are now in Christ, not solely on who we used to be.

3 Leading with integrity

1 Timothy 2:8—3:13

These are difficult verses. Whether you are more egalitarian or complementarian, whether you're a woman or not, the instructions here for women to be 'quiet' are strikingly countercultural in today's world. The word count I have is inadequate for any substantial analysis of gender roles as presented in 1 Timothy and the New Testament more broadly. But, instead of doing a woeful job of textual analysis, I want to point us to a broader theme we encounter in these verses, one that may help us understand the tricky verses: Paul is demanding integrity from those who will carry forward the gospel message.

Church leadership is difficult. This is as true now as it was then, even if the situations faced are markedly different. One thing I imagine has remained the same, though, is fallible humans trying to display the goodness of an infallible God. To do this well, the whole body of Christ needs to be involved because we each bring different gifts to the table (see 1 Corinthians 12). But we also need leaders who can teach doctrine and scripture, who can provide pastoral care and direct the path of the church they have been given. Church leaders aren't innately better people than their laity. God doesn't love them more or grant them special blessings reserved for the select few. However, leaders do have responsibilities marked out for them in passages like today's.

Paul's instructions here rely upon the integrity of the leader. Paul wants church leaders to be well-respected and well-liked, not because church leadership is a popularity contest but because the gospel can't spread when its teachers are selfish or distracted. Perhaps the reason why Paul wants the women in Ephesus to be modestly dressed and quiet is because their current behaviour detracts people from the gospel message they are purporting to teach. Remember that Paul's first admonition to Timothy regards false teachers. The call to 'practise what you preach' comes to mind. When our church leaders talk and behave in ways that seem contrary to the gospel, we lose faith in them and sometimes even in the church entirely.

So it is important, however we understand the gender roles being outlined here, to remember that every church leader's first call is to follow Jesus themselves. If they're not doing so, they cannot credibly instruct others to do the same.

4 Rejecting hypocrisy

1 Timothy 3:14—4:5

We are brought back to Genesis in these verses, with Paul reminding the church in Ephesus (via Timothy) that creation is good, with a specific emphasis here on food. Oftentimes at the moment, when we discuss creation theologically, the priority is often environmentalism. How can we protect the natural world? This is a good and worthwhile endeavour, one we must spend more time on. But that is not necessarily what Paul is referring to here.

The forbidding of marriage and abstaining from certain foods were characteristic of sects led by 'hypocritical liars' (4:2). When considered alongside the other warnings regarding false teachings, it can be assumed that Paul is concerned about the motivations of the teachers and the ways that it can distract people from Jesus.

Despite the inclusion of marriage in these verses being a source of interest for many readers, it is more appropriate to understand these verses as being about food. We can infer from these verses (with knowledge of the historical context) that the leaders Paul refers to enforced harsh dietary restrictions on their followers, even though Jesus (and later Peter) had asserted that there needn't be further delineations regarding clean and unclean foods. But, as with the earlier discussion about false teachings, this is not a critique of people trying their best to understand the changes to their religious activity and getting confused. Paul is calling out these leaders for their deceptive ways.

Interestingly, this passage sits between two passages discussing qualities of good leadership. Paul is constantly keeping Timothy aware of possible traps he may fall into, or that he should identify in others. Consistency is crucial to good Christian leadership. Paul is not condemning abstaining from particular foods or even abstaining from marriage. He is condemning a more systemic issue in the leadership of those sects: hypocrisy.

Hypocrisy in leadership shouldn't come as a surprise to Timothy and it shouldn't to us either. Paul writes that people will go astray and deviate from Christ's teaching. We could debate endlessly what that means and what that looks like, but the important thing to note here is that the church is 'the pillar and foundation of the truth' (3:15) and so it ought to be respected as such.

5 Practising godliness

1 Timothy 4:6—5:2

Those who run will know that the first run (or the first run in a while) can feel like it lasts a lifetime – even if it only lasts a mere number of minutes. But, as your body becomes more adjusted to moving in such a way, it becomes easier and easier. Soon, what once felt like a lifetime is now a warm-up jog on a much longer run.

Practising godliness is somewhat similar. It can be easy to assume that being godly is a sort of 'automatic upgrade' that one receives upon becoming a Christian. Or, if not when someone becomes a Christian, surely when one is appointed to lead. But Paul's instructions to Timothy here indicate that practising godliness is not as simple as it may seem. By likening it to 'physical training' (v. 8), Paul is pointing us to the reality that godliness is not found in quick fixes or by taking shortcuts.

As Paul says, 'godliness has value for all things' (4:8) and therefore it is a noble goal for each of us. However, just as skipping to the fourth week of a running programme isn't wise, so too should we be mindful that racing ahead in our journey with godliness isn't wise either. It takes practice, so we cannot beat ourselves up when we falter. And we shouldn't necessarily set the same expectations on new Christians as we do on seasoned leaders. Paul speaks of the church seeing Timothy's 'progress' (4:15). It is not a shameful thing to grow; it is a sign of the Spirit working within us.

It is common to hear 4:12 used to uplift young leaders in the church. It is worth remembering, though, that this is not necessarily optimal. We should not rely on our young people to 'set an example for the believers in speech, in conduct, in love, in faith and in purity' (4:12). It is wonderful when they do so and we should honour and respect the words of our youth. But hopefully, we can also provide positive role models for them too, from all generations. 1 Timothy so far has largely been about false and hypocritical leaders. Perhaps the church in Ephesus needed young leaders like Timothy because they had no good ones from older generations. Let us not fall into a similar trap, relying on youth because they could not rely on us.

6 Uplifting the downtrodden

1 Timothy 5:3–16

'Fighting the battle' for Christ is not always about being on the offensive. There are defence mechanisms that the church needs to properly implement if it is to be the most successful in the battle. These are outlined in our reading today. Paul acknowledges that sometimes vulnerable people (with a specific focus here on young widowed women) draw away from Christ as they seek to elevate their status or fix their situation (v. 11). Therefore, supporting the vulnerable is not just an inclusionary measure; it's a way of protecting the spiritual life of the flock.

Offensive and defensive strategies are equally valuable in military campaigns or team sports, even if the offensive plays tend to get more attention from those looking on. Just because a player isn't scoring goals doesn't mean they don't work as hard as the others on the team. Likewise, working to care for the vulnerable in a church family may not be a glamorous role. It'll likely involve a lot of hard work that is largely hidden. But it is stressed throughout scripture that God calls his people to care for the vulnerable. It is an important part of the church's DNA.

Why then does Paul delineate who can and cannot receive institutional support? Consider your own church. It may long to serve everyone, but the desires of the church body are often (sadly) overwhelmed by the great needs of the wider community. And, even if there were endless resources, it is extremely difficult to be 'all things for all people'. Paul isn't establishing a hierarchy of care, although it can certainly appear that way at first glance. He's acknowledging that the church doesn't have infinite capacity. So, if there are people within the church community who can support their own relatives, they ought to do that first, ensuring that those with truly nothing can access the care they need.

Guidelines

In this first week of notes, I have outlined some of the ways I see Paul instructing Timothy to build on his existing good work and grow as a leader. Wherever your relationship is to leadership, here are some questions to consider:

- Where are you? Some of us have been told to stay where we are, whereas others of us are called to move on. I find that not engaging the question regularly can lead to complacency. We stay in the same place (if not physically, then spiritually) because it's often easier to do so. So, first and foremost, locate yourself. Consider where you are and perhaps even ask God if you ought to stay there.
- Throughout 1 and 2 Timothy, Paul instructs Timothy to cling to gospel truths and defend them. How do you ensure that you know these for yourself? Is it through regular Bible reading, engagement in a church community, or are there other ways you remind yourself of God's goodness?
- What is your testimony? Recall your journey of faith and consider how God may be prompting you to lead and serve others in the way only you can. Each of us has unique gifts and abilities, but we also each have a unique story, which can sometimes be just as powerful a tool for mission and ministry as our tangible skills.
- Paul tells Timothy to reject hypocrisy. Where do you see hypocrisy most clearly in your world? Perhaps it's your workplace or community, or maybe it's through the news when you look at national and international leaders. Consider where hypocrisy may be seeping into your own heart and ask God to convict you of where you may be able to change.
- Uplifting the downtrodden was a crucial part of Jesus' mission and therefore ought to be replicated in our ministry today. How might you engage in your community to care more for the vulnerable among you, even if and when they pose challenges?

1 Respecting authority

1 Timothy 5:17—6:2

There are two ways that Paul instructs us to treat authority in this passage, and both must be held together. First, respect those appointed to church leadership, and second, those leaders must respect the office they've been given.

That second piece is sadly often neglected in conversations surrounding accountability and the discipline of leaders. Too many of us have experienced being told to respect authority even though the authority figure in question is perhaps undeserving of our respect. Paul is clear, though, especially considering 1 and 2 Timothy as a whole, that Christian leadership is a position that demands great effort as well as significant sacrifice.

Christian leaders, then and now, are put on the spot, held to higher standards and frequently criticised and scrutinised for every little thing they say or do. Paul is mindful to tell Timothy that he needs to support his fellow leaders, likely because accusations will come and they need to be responded to reasonably and fairly. However, Paul does not tell Timothy that there are never to be repercussions. Elders found to be sinning are to be charged publicly 'so that the others may take warning' (5:20). They are removed from their post because they did not respect the position of authority they had been given.

As discussed in last week's notes, integrity is of the utmost importance to Paul because of the implications it has for the advancement of the gospel. Even regarding the treatment of slaves, Paul is clear about the reasons for respecting authority. Enslaved people should respect their masters so that 'God's name and our teaching may not be slandered' (6:1). As with the passages on gender last week, there is too little space here for me to unpack all the implications of Paul's instructions to slaves, and I appreciate that these verses were used to punish those fighting for their freedom.

However, I still think there could be value to this message when we understand the broader context of the passage. There are instructions here for the enslaved and the enslavers. The expectation implicitly stated is that Christian masters ought to treat their slaves better than those who did not believe. Those in any form of authority ought to be able to be charged with doing the same. We need to respect the authority we've been given, not just the people under whose authority we sit.

2 Setting good priorities

1 Timothy 6:2–21

The New Testament contains numerous seemingly harsh words about money, including these verses at the end of 1 Timothy. ‘The love of money is a root of all kinds of evil,’ writes Paul (v. 10). Once again, scripture is imploring us to consider our priorities. As has surely been said before and will surely be said again, it’s not that money is in itself bad, it’s just that it can consume our hearts and minds such that we cannot keep our eyes fixed on Jesus. After all, as Jesus says himself, ‘you cannot serve both God and Money’ (Matthew 6:24).

Paul is worried that the church may become distracted, with some becoming tempted by the material wealth on offer in Ephesus. By its positioning in the letter, Paul’s instruction here relates the love of money to the ease with which some follow (or indeed promote) false teaching. Both are distractions and detract from the life that can be found in Christ, and Christ alone. So Paul tells Timothy to ‘flee from all this, and pursue righteousness, godliness, faith, love, endurance and gentleness’ (v. 11).

And so, it is therefore wise to associate Paul’s teachings here with Jesus’ teachings on money, specifically Matthew 6:19–21 which concludes with the phrase, ‘for where your treasure is, there your heart will be also’. If one’s heart is in Christ and not in the false teachings rife around them, they will have stored treasures in heaven. They will be content and will not stray from the faith (as verse 10 warns against).

The same admonition can be given to us today. While it may not always seem like it and while it may not reach every corner of the world equally, I imagine that wealth is as pervasive a temptation for us today as it was for Timothy’s congregation in Ephesus. Translators debate if the love of money as described in verse 10 is ‘the root’ of evil or ‘a root’ (thus implying that there can be other sources of evil). Regardless, it seems fair to say that when people are ‘eager for money’ above all else, selfishness ensues and ‘ruin and destruction’ are inevitable. We are not to condemn those who ‘fall into temptation’ (v. 9) but instead, envelop them back into the fold of God and show them the abundant life found in Christ.

3 Living in community

2 Timothy 1:1–12

The second letter opens with Paul reflecting on the impact of Timothy's family's faith, specifically the positive influence of his mother and grandmother. By the time Paul is writing 2 Timothy, he is towards the end of his life and thus perhaps pondering his own legacy. He looks to the lineage of Lois, Eunice and then Timothy, and sees the joy found in experiencing the Christian life together in community, particularly a familial community – one he may not have had. But, while Paul may not have had a Christian heritage, he certainly leaves behind a legacy of faith in Jesus, with Timothy playing a significant part in that.

Paul and Timothy are close. Paul recalls Timothy's tears and, while we do not know why Timothy cried before Paul, his expressed vulnerability reveals the depth of their mutual fellowship. True vulnerability in relationships is rare, particularly nowadays among male friendships. Embedded in Paul's personal note of comfort to Timothy is a reminder to all of us that being open and honest in our relationships is significant. Living in a community of faith necessitates that we share openly, such that we can build one another up in love. In this regard, while Paul praises the familial line of faith found in Lois, Eunice and Timothy, Paul demonstrates that the encouragement found in Christian heritage is not restricted to bloodlines. Timothy is indeed the perfect example of this. The book of Acts tells us that while he was the son of 'a believer' (Acts 16:1), Timothy's father was Greek. It was Paul who took Timothy to be circumcised, not his own father, as would have been customary. Mentorship is as strong a bond as any.

Yet, the possible absence of Timothy's father does not negate the example set by his maternal line, a faith that Paul declares 'now lives in [Timothy] also' (v. 5). Faith cannot be inherited. However, strong role models in the faith (whether they are family members like Lois and Eunice, or mentors like Paul) are so important for a person's growth and discipleship. Paul remarks later that Timothy had learned the scriptures 'from infancy' (3:15). What greater encouragement do we need to spur us on to teach our youth and children the fundamentals of our faith? We are called not just to be in community with those like us, but to be an intergenerational family that is raising up the next generations of believers.

4 Finding hope in suffering

2 Timothy 1:13—2:13

This letter to Timothy continues with a discussion on suffering, in which Paul refers to the trials he is undertaking for the sake of the 'elect' so that they may 'obtain… salvation' (2:10). Here, Paul does not explicitly state that Timothy is experiencing suffering. But it is fair to imagine that Timothy would have taken great comfort in Paul's words as he navigated church leadership. Paul even invites Timothy to 'join with me in suffering, like a good soldier of Christ Jesus' (2:3).

Whether a Christian must suffer to truly walk with Christ is a debated topic. Some tend towards a prosperity gospel in which God bestows blessings on those who serve his church, whereas others claim almost the opposite: that suffering is a crucial element of the Christian life. Jesus himself says the infamous words, 'Whoever wants to be my disciple must deny themselves and take up their cross and follow me' (Matthew 16:24), a verse that has been used to justify and explain the sufferings of Christians throughout history.

Paul's assessment, as explored in this part of 2 Timothy, seems to be that suffering is a natural byproduct of trying to walk with Christ. In 2:4–6, Paul speaks of the hard work that comes when striving to be a good disciple. Pleasing one's commanding officer – to use the analogy from 2:4 – would have won a soldier favour with their superior but could have led to frustration from their peers. The important thing, Paul seems to be saying, is that a follower of Christ needs to keep their eyes fixed on their prize as an athlete focuses on the 'victor's crown' (2:5).

But, while there are challenges, there is hope for Paul because 'God's word is not chained' (2:9) and because he believes his suffering is for the 'eternal glory' (2:10) of others. The suffering we may undergo as Christians in the western world will likely be minimal compared to what others around the world experience. But we can all rely on the 'trustworthy saying' Paul points us to, one that begins: 'If we died with him, we will also live with him' (2:11). Suffering is only temporary and can bring life to someone else, but ultimately, the reward is eternal glory with Christ. Therefore, there is reason to hope.

5 Instructing with gentleness

2 Timothy 2:14—3:9

Paul is clear with Timothy: 'The Lord's servant must not be quarrelsome but must be kind to everyone, able to teach, not resentful' (2:24). The placement of these three qualities together is interesting, with the inclusion of an ability to teach indicating that Paul is likely referring to those who serve in church leadership. While seemingly random, these three traits summarise much of what Paul has said about leadership thus far in the letters to Timothy. Leadership is about servanthood first and foremost, and it is important for a church leader to have a good reputation in the community in order to be trusted by the people. Kindness remains underrated, but a habitual lack of it is a sure way to lose respect. And thus, it is not just that one must be able to teach well to be an effective leader; one must do so with kindness and without bitterness.

These principles can be applied broadly, whether one is in church leadership and whether one is actively teaching or not. Consider 2:25–26. We are to 'gently [instruct]' our opponents 'in the hope that God will grant them repentance'. It is not our responsibility to change the mind of a stern adversary; it is the work of the Holy Spirit. However, Paul knows that aggressive rebukes and harsh words hardly help. It's a familiar phrase, but it's certainly in line with the gospel to say that 'a small act of kindness can go a long way'. We must not underestimate how even our minor moments of unkindness can turn people away from the gospel.

Perhaps this is why Paul identifies so clearly the traits of those who have rejected the gospel (3:1–5). Paul tells Timothy to steer clear of people who act in ways antithetical to the gospel so that he is not influenced negatively. And while true that ultimately, 'their folly will be clear to everyone' (3:9), our world is so filled with folly that it can sometimes be hard to distinguish between those with good gospel-centred intentions and those without. We ought to check ourselves against Paul's list as well as seek to avoid those who demonstrate such qualities.

Living in kindness and gentleness isn't always easy, particularly when it feels like our opponents are gaining ground. But Paul knows that a pure heart is the best way to reflect Christ's redeeming love to a broken world.

6 Learning from scripture

2 Timothy 3:10—4:22

Perhaps the most famous teaching from 2 Timothy is found in this passage, that 'all Scripture is God-breathed and is useful for teaching, rebuking, correcting and training in righteousness, so that the servant of God may be thoroughly equipped for every good work' (3:16–17). It is a debated passage among Christians because of the various ways one can interpret scripture as 'God-breathed' and what that means in terms of how we should apply it. As I conclude these notes on the two epistles to Timothy, it seems pertinent to focus on how we learn from scripture as a means to better walk through the world as followers of Jesus.

Scripture is useful. Presumably, you have already bought into this as someone reading Bible notes! But the thing I find striking when reading verses 16 and 17 in context is that Paul is praising Timothy's commitment to the scriptures from infancy – a reminder of his faithful family. Surely Paul is referring to Timothy's Old Testament knowledge, as that's what would have been his holy text. (The New Testament wasn't canonised until later.) And so, in our own teaching and reading today, we must also be instructed by the Old Testament. My experience has been that the majority of a church's sermon content comes from the New Testament (even in circumstances when a lectionary is used) or from familiar Old Testament books. There is an invitation from Paul to teach all of it, even from childhood. We may not deem every story appropriate for our Sunday school classes, but teaching the next generation how to engage well with the Bible seems of great importance, as it is how we will equip them for 'every good work' (3:17).

After reminding Timothy of the lessons he has taught him throughout the letter, Paul closes with a fond farewell, noting that he has 'fought the good fight' and 'finished the race' (4:7). It is noteworthy that Paul, looking back at the end of his life, marvels at Timothy's commitment to the scriptures. We know that Paul was a highly religious Jew before his encounter with Christ; he likely knew the scriptures very well also. But Paul identifies this as something that distinguishes Timothy and makes him a good leader. So let us follow Timothy's example in being people who dwell in Spirit and in truth (John 4:24).

Guidelines

This second week of notes has given further guidance for leaders but also provided some general principles for living well together in Christian community. Here are some questions to consider:

- What authority have you been given? Even if you do not hold a named position of leadership in your workplace/community/church, God has given you people over whom you have some influence. How might you steward that well this week?
- Reflect on your family tree, both your biological one and your spiritual one. What lessons have you learned from each of these trees, and which are the lessons you would most like to pass on to the next generation? Consider how you may invest in someone younger than you, as Paul did for Timothy. Remember that they do not need to be your own biological children for you to have a significant impact on their development.
- How might you study the scriptures more so that you can instruct with gentleness and be a good witness to the grace found in Jesus' message?

FURTHER READING

Osvaldo Padilla, *The Pastoral Epistles: An introduction and commentary* (Tyndale, 2022).

Eugene Peterson, *Eat This Book: A conversation in the art of spiritual reading* (Hodder & Stoughton, 2011).

Tom Wright, *Paul for Everyone: The pastoral letters* (SPCK, 2014).

Isaiah of Jerusalem

Henry Wansbrough

God called Abraham to be a nomad and led him into the slip of land on the eastern shore of the Mediterranean. In search of food, his descendants went down to Egypt, where they became a mighty people. When God led them out of Egypt through the desert of Sinai for 40 years, they had a unique experience of becoming God's special people, under divine protection and guided by divine Law. But they were unfaithful to the divine covenant, flirting with other gods, particularly the fertility gods of the land into which the Lord had led them.

Then the great empires of Mesopotamia, first Assyria and later Babylon, expanded westwards and threatened to engulf them. Despite the warnings of the prophets Amos and Hosea, they refused to rely on the Lord for protection and turned to other political alliances. The northern part of the territory of Israel was swallowed up by Assyria. A major part of its population, ten tribes, was deported to other parts of the Assyrian Empire in 730BC and disappears from history. Not unlike the present day, it looked as though true religion might be swamped by the 'godless' powers of Mesopotamia. Prophets were sent to assure believers that true religion would triumph. If they held firm, the Lord would protect his own.

In 740BC, Isaiah of Jerusalem was called to give God's warning to Judah and Jerusalem. He warned them that they would be driven into exile, though his son was to be called 'Shear Yashub' ('a Remnant will Return'). This forms the book of Emmanuel (chapters 1—12). It is followed by threats against the hostile nations. A second major part of the book of Isaiah (chapters 40—55) foretells the return from exile decreed by King Cyrus in the year 538BC. A third section follows (chapters 56—66), proclaimed mostly after the return from Exile. In these two weeks we will be reflecting on the first part (1—39), the most authentic prophecies of Isaiah.

Bible quotations are taken from the NRSV.

1 The call of Isaiah

Isaiah 6

Isaiah's call sets the tone for the whole book of Isaiah. It was an awesome experience and provides the key to his concept of God, whom he calls 'the Lord', 'the King', 'the Lord Sabaoth', and most of all 'the Holy One of Israel'. This awesome presence is the background of all Isaiah's thinking, his reverence, his fear and his longing.

'Holy, holy, holy' will return in the final book of the Bible, the Revelation to John, in the glorious vision of the heavenly court (Revelation 4:8). It is sung continuously, night and day, by the four living creatures with six wings, a hymn of thanksgiving for creation. There, in its Christian modification, the Lamb that seemed to have been sacrificed stands in the middle of the throne and shares the worship given to the One sitting on the throne.

Isaiah's reaction is an acute awareness of his own sinfulness by comparison. But his lips are cleansed by the burning coal taken from the altar, and he responds, 'Here I am.' It is the response of all God's messengers, from Abraham (Genesis 22:1) to Mary at the Annunciation (Luke 1:38) and Paul on the road to Damascus (Acts 9). It is the response put by the letter to the Hebrews on the lips of Jesus, 'Here I am. I have come to do your will' (Hebrews 10:7–10), the prelude to his willing sacrifice made once and for all. Some try to avoid the call, like Moses at the burning bush, who protests his inadequacy, or Jeremiah, who claims he can only stammer like a child. Jonah even tries to run away (Jonah 1:3). The task of being God's messenger brings pain and persecution; it is not to be lightly undertaken.

This brings us up against the mystery of God's gift of free will. Right at the beginning of his mission, Isaiah is warned that they will not respond. Even God cannot compel us to respond. The frustration is built into the message of Jesus, 'so that they may look and look but not see, may listen and listen but not understand' (Mark 4:12). It is hammered home at the end of Acts by Paul in Rome. The Christian claims to respond to the call. Where do I stand?

2 A disaster situation

Isaiah 1:2–28

Isaiah's message begins, in the present arrangement of his prophecies – and, of course, the arrangement was put together long after the prophet's time – with dissatisfaction. These verses may well be entirely from Isaiah himself. Its purpose is to give a clear picture of Israel's disastrous fall, despite the nation's glorious destiny. It falls into three clearly independent sections.

The first major section (vv. 2–9), by its allusion to the multiple wounds of the country, and especially the situation of Jerusalem/Zion, should date from the time of the devastation of the country in 701BC by the Assyrian king Sennacherib. It is a statement of the bruised and endangered condition of Israel. There are three powerful images. The contrast between the mute, affectionate, unquestioning loyalty of the ox and ass and the treacherous rebelliousness of the children of the Holy One of Israel has, from the time of Francis of Assisi, won its place in our Christian crib-scenes, emphasising the contrast between the worshipping welcome of Gentile wise men and the murderous malice of the Jewish king. The second image, disease and suppurating sores, needs neither emphasis nor explanation. The third image, a shanty in a vineyard or a hut in a cucumber field, evokes one upstanding structure amid ground-hugging plants, such as one still sees in the fields of cucumber, melon and tomato in the Galilean plain. It dates the prophecy probably to the occasion of the Assyrian invasion in 701BC, when archaeology confirms that all the outlying towns of Judah were sacked, leaving only Jerusalem untouched. After some sabre-rattling at the gates of Jerusalem, recorded in Isaiah 36—37, the Assyrian army mysteriously withdrew. This could be explained only as divine intervention.

The second section (vv. 10–20), now linked on by the catchphrase 'Sodom and Gomorrah', specifies the futility of religious ritual without moral and social justice in the manner of the earlier prophets of the northern kingdom, but also of Micah in the southern kingdom of Judah. It takes the form of a triple summons (vv. 10, 16, 18) to enter into a judicial discussion of true justice.

The third section (vv. 21–28) is a lament, bracketed by the electrifying keywords 'fair judgement', 'faithful', 'saving justice', constituting a fierce contrast between what is and what should be. It is written in the mourning rhythm of laments, three stresses, followed by two stresses in each line.

3 The song of the vineyard

Isaiah 5

This lovely song is built on a song of the grape-harvest. It is, of course, a major toil to set up a vineyard. The stony ground must first be cleared. If it is on a hillside, the stones will be used to build terraces horizontally along the contour-lines of the hill, to prevent the earth being washed down by the rains in winter, for soil erosion by the rains is a major problem in the hill-country of Israel. The watchtower is there to prevent the harvesting of the grapes by thieves and will be manned night and day during the ripening season. A winepress on the spot shows the thoughtful planning and care that has been taken, for damage to grapes during transport in bullock-carts is all too easy. Obviously it is both easier and less wasteful to transport the grape-juice rather than risking loss by the transport of the fresh grapes themselves. This is a complete and well-appointed wine-making business, and truly every care has been taken. But it still has to be tended lovingly, especially in the skilled and delicate operations of pruning and harvesting the grapes.

The continuous care demanded for a successful vineyard makes the image of the Lord's vineyard ideal for Israel. It was used already by Hosea 10 with the connotations of a vineyard which has got out of control and needs vigorous pruning, or even hacking back, curbing the excesses which had sprouted in Israel. Jeremiah will use it too, as does Isaiah here, to complain of the mutations that have occurred in the fruit: the best vines planted, but producing only inferior fruit. Isaiah expresses it by means of a double pun in verse 7: the Lord expected *mishpat* (just judgements) but found only *mispah* (bloodshed); he expected *zedaqah* (righteousness) but found only *ze'aqah* (a cry of distress).

Jesus, in his turn, uses the figure in his parable of the wicked vinedressers (Matthew 21:33–41), who look after the Lord's vineyard but refuse to yield its fruit, alluding so clearly to the passage of Isaiah that the leaders of Israel cannot miss the criticism of themselves and finally decide to do away with Jesus. Finally, John gives us the image of the true vine (John 15). Jesus is the real vine prefigured by the vine of Israel. The tendrils must draw life from him if they are to bear fruit.

4 The virgin is with child

Isaiah 7

We must consider this well-loved passage on two levels: the original context and the use made of it. The original context is preparations for war. In 736BC King Ahaz of Judah is preparing a water-channel to bring the water-supply from outside the city into the inside of the city, so that his capital can withstand siege by his two enemies Pekah, king of Israel, and Razon, king of Syria (or Aram). The successor to this channel still exists.

Ahaz prefers to rely on his own resourcefulness. Isaiah insists that true security comes only from the Lord. But what is the sign he proffers? It cannot primarily be the Messiah, for the sign must be a sign to Ahaz. Some have seen the prophecy as an assurance that Ahaz's pregnant wife will give birth to a male child. The difficulty about this is that we know of no male child born to Ahaz in that year, and the royal records are usually quite full on this matter. Others see it as a time-signal, for the pregnant woman is unnamed: before a woman now pregnant has time to give birth, the invading armies will have collapsed. This makes good sense, and indeed the alliance against Assyria soon collapsed, but the annoyance to Assyria was enough to provoke them to invade the kingdom of Samaria. The consequences of this are described as a plague of killer-bees, given immediacy by the quadruple repetition of 'that day' in verses 18, 20, 21 and 22.

The original Hebrew speaks only of a 'a young woman', not necessarily a virgin. It is only the Greek translation of the Bible, made two centuries before Christ, which uses the word *Parthenos*, which carries the sense of a fresh young girl, normally a woman sexually inexperienced. This is the text used by the gospel of Matthew to show that Jesus' birth from the virgin Mary was a fulfilment of scripture. Some say that Isaiah, filled with the spirit of prophecy, said more than he intended. Others use the choice of the word by the translators as evidence that they too were led by the Spirit of God to choose it, and so enlarge the sense which was not present in the original prophecy. This would be one more evidence of the gradual revelation of God's purposes in the scriptures, and of the divine guardianship of the scriptures throughout the history of the people of God.

5 A promise of deliverance

Isaiah 9:1—10:4

The prophecy in 9:1–6 combines a promise of liberty and restoration after misery with a promise of a transcendent monarchy for Judah. The language used echoes the promise made to David by his prophet Nathan in 2 Samuel 7 but enlarges it on to a wider or even a transcendent plane. The tone is reminiscent of Egyptian coronation hymns which, like Psalms 2 and 110 in the Davidic tradition, speak of the birth of the king to a deity or his adoption by the deity; hymns announcing the divine sonship of the king seem to have been part of the accession-ritual; the king is spoken of as either born to or adopted by the god. The passage is hard to date and has been attached to the coronation of both Hezekiah and Josiah. Only in the former case would it be genuinely from Isaiah. Each of them was hailed as introducing a new era of fidelity and prosperity after the disastrous and unfaithful conduct of their predecessors.

The names given are presumably throne-names, designating the functions and success of the monarch, for it was Egyptian practice to give five throne-names; in this case one would have dropped out. The question is how literally the language and imagery are intended: in the language of this tradition the king at least stands in the place of God, and it is hard to see in what sense the expressions 'Mighty God' (possibly to be translated 'Divine Warrior') and 'Eternal Father' can be attenuated onto the level of anything merely human. To say that Isaiah is using the conventions of court-language does not remove the far-reaching overtones of the promise of a ruler here made. And even though the poem may originally have been composed to celebrate the birth or accession of King Hezekiah or Josiah, their achievement and personality do not exhaust its potential; the far-reaching promises made still foreshadow an even greater future for the kingly line of David. Is this already a prophecy of the incarnation? This may be another case (like the virgin birth) where Christians understand literally what the original author did not fully intend.

None of the official Jewish translations into Greek translate the Hebrew as 'Mighty God'; seemingly this would be considered blasphemous. They use language more Messianic than divine. The official Septuagint has, 'messenger/angel of wondrous counsel, for I shall bring peace to the rulers, peace and health to them', though the Targum (the first-century Jewish explanation) goes so far as to give 'wondrous counsellor, mighty God'.

6 A promise of restoration

Isaiah 11

The group of prophecies of the restoration after the exile, often known as the book of Emmanuel, sums up and concludes with this poem, probably dated towards the end of the exile in Babylon. The poem, particularly the emphasis on the Spirit, is used liberally in Christian liturgies centred on the gift of the Spirit. The poem is the basis of the traditional seven gifts of the Spirit. This gift of the Spirit of the Lord here delineated through the return of the House of David features prominently throughout the Bible, but especially in the post-exilic literature. At the very beginning the Spirit of the Lord hovers over the waters at the creation and gives life (Genesis 1). It is a Spirit of power which seizes upon the Judges to direct them in God's way. Again the Spirit or breath of the Lord gives new life to Israel at the return of the people after the exile (Ezekiel 37). It inspires the leaders of God's people, such as the Judges, and especially King Saul, and all the leaders of God's people. It gives craftsmen their skills and Joseph his wisdom in Egypt.

The gift of the Spirit at the renewal of Israel is one of the themes which draw together the three different parts of the prophecies of Isaiah. In the second part of Isaiah possession of the Spirit is one of the major characteristics of the servant of the Lord (42:1). In the final, triumphant poems the messenger of the Lord is anointed with the Spirit (61:1), just as the Holy Spirit has guided them throughout their history (63:11–14). In the present poem the emphasis is on the governing and guiding sevenfold Spirit of wisdom and power exercised by the promised descendant of David. The peace brought by the shoot from the stock of Jesse will extend to the animal kingdom so that natural enmities and harmfulness will be quelled, and perfect peace will reign.

All this is, of course, a preparation for the understanding of the Spirit as the Advocate or Helper, sent by the Father and the Son, filling, guiding God's people and bringing them to perfection, as promised and revealed in the New Testament.

Guidelines

Starting with and suffused by the glimpse of the majesty of the Lord all holy, this first part of the proclamation of Isaiah is full of contradiction: Jerusalem is 'like a hut in a cucumber field', alone upright amid the devastation wreaked by Sennacherib. And yet, the promise to the line of David stands firm: Emmanuel, God with us; he will establish an era of peace and prosperity which will extend to the whole of creation. There is even a glimmering that this prince will be more than human, the representative of the Lord in a new creation filled with the Spirit of the Lord.

Questions for reflection:

- Have you or has anyone you know ever received a direct experience of God?
- How do we normally get to know God's will?
- Is there any equivalent of prophecy in today's world?
- How does the Holy Spirit guide your ministry?
- Does the Holy Spirit work through the enemies of God?

1 Prophecies against the nations

Isaiah 13

The book of Emmanuel ended with a prophecy of the scattered exiles being gathered in at the end of the exile, followed by a psalm-like hymn of thanksgiving. Then follows a collection of proclamations against the surrounding nations and their unsuccessful attempts to rid themselves of the yoke of the great empires of Assyria and Babylon. The chief lesson of these is the unassailable power of the Lord who controls the whole of history. Many of these are impossible to date, and are certainly later than the historic mission of the prophet Isaiah of Jerusalem, starting in the 740s BC. They are gathered into the book of Isaiah as a sort of legacy of the prophet.

The most magnificent of these poems of the wars of the Lord of Hosts – for that is the warlike title under which the Lord makes war (v. 4; 14:22–27; 18:7; 19:12–25, etc) – is this first one. Much of the poem is couched in the general language of the horror of wars, the slaughter of children, the desolation of the landscape, the unchecked ravaging of odious and frightening wild beasts such as wildcats, hyenas and jackals. This is shared with later descriptions, such as Jeremiah 50—51. It is not until near the end of the poem that a focus on Babylon appears (vv. 17–19). It will be taken up by the taunt-song on the King of Babylon in the following chapter. The actual record of the capture of Babylon by the Medes on the Cyrus Cylinder, contemporaneously crafted in 538BC, describes the attackers as 'strolling in, their weapons packed away', but this no doubt was not literal but expressed the victors' boast of the ease of their conquest.

The poem reflects the vivid technicolour of the Day of the Lord, the destined and terrible day when the Lord will put all things to rights, already invoked by the prophet Amos 8:9. It will be a frightening day when nature itself will be thrown into confusion, a day of cosmic horror, when even sun, moon and stars refuse to perform their appointed functions, a day of punishment for wickedness, pride and arrogance. Once this atmosphere of horror and impotence at the divine punishment has been established, it suffuses the fragmentary instances of the punishment of smaller nations as they writhe and struggle for liberation from the fist of the great empires, first of Assyria, then of Babylon. The dread of that day is vividly expressed in Isaiah 21.

2 Punishment and reward

Isaiah 24

This section of Isaiah, chapters 24—27, used to be called 'The Apocalypse of Isaiah', a useful term though confusing, for sometimes the expression 'apocalyptic literature' is also used to designate those books of the Bible which were written in Greek, not Hebrew, and for this reason were separated off by the Lutheran tradition as not quite fully inspired. The title 'Apocalypse' means 'Revelation', and the apocalyptic literature reveals its message by means of heavenly happenings which have their equivalent on earth, battles between the forces of good and of evil which are reflected on earth, often with the turmoil of strife in heaven and chaos among the stars and in the solar system. This vivid form of writing is here not yet fully developed; it became very widespread in Judaism in the final three centuries before Christ, e.g. Daniel 12, the Book of Henoch, the Dead Sea Scrolls. In the New Testament it occurs in the chapters such as Mark 13, where the coming of the Son of Man at the end of the world is being described, as well as in the final book of the Bible, the book of Revelation or Apocalypse. In our passage it occurs in verses 18–22.

Principally, however, our passage sums up the doom-laden prophecies of disaster on the small and prosperous states, trading-cities such as Ashdod and Tyre, afflicted by the advance of the great empires of Assyria and Babylon. This is summed up at last in disaster to Babylon itself, though the name of the city is not actually given: the creation-process is itself set in reverse: the Lord does not create a garden but lays the earth waste; its inhabitants are scattered, as at the Tower of Babel; it becomes a city of nothingness, a non-city, with the earth reeling to and fro like a drunkard and the sun ashamed. This prophetic description of destruction stands in sharp contrast to the historical description (in the contemporary 'Cyrus Cylinder') of the assailants marching into proud Babylon with their weapons tucked away. In Isaiah, all the stress is on the power of the Lord: the earth cracks open, but psalms can be heard, 'Glory to the Righteous one'. The destruction stands in sharp contrast to the encouraging description of the eschatological banquet for Jerusalem which follows in 25:6–8.

3 A diptych: destruction or salvation

Isaiah 34—35

The imagery of the war in heaven, the sky rolled up like a scroll and the Lord's sword sated with blood (34:4–6) has earned these chapters the title, 'Isaiah's Little Apocalypse'. The enemy, the source and embodiment of all evil, is symbolised and often personified by different nations in the course of biblical history. In the long and drawn-out period of the prophet Isaiah, the enemy is first Assyria, then Babylon and finally Edom.

Where within the final period of the Second Temple these two chapters fall it is impossible to say, for the roots of rivalry between Israel and Edom go back to the tribal legends of Jacob/Israel and Esau/Edom in Genesis 25. The present chapters have been dated by various scholars to the fifth or fourth centuries, or even later. Edom remained Israel's enemy even into the Second Temple period, continually encroaching from the south, taking over more and more of the Negev desert. Much of the blessing on Israel in chapter 35 is echoed in Isaiah 40—55, particularly the image of the straight highway of return to Zion, with which the poem ends (35:10). This contrast, and the triumphant promises for Jerusalem, conclude the prophetic and poetic part of the first part of Isaiah, separated from the Second Part by the historical accounts of King Hezekiah.

Psalm 137, while already a tragic song about the desolation of the psalmists of Israel at their abandonment in Babylon, is infected at the end by a prayer for murderous revenge on the children of Edom, who had somehow taken part in the siege and destruction of Jerusalem. The siege had ended with massive deportations and executions. That was the style of the time; the Moabite Stone (a victory inscription of about 830BC) records that the King of Moab after a victory slaughtered seven thousand men, women and children to his god. The hostility between the two nations continues here. The Lord's sword will fall on Edom (34:5; see also 63:1). The two chapters 34 and 35 are two sides of one coin: a curse for Edom, a blessing for Jerusalem: no travel for Edom, a highway for Israel (34:10; 35:8); streams of pitch for Edom, water for Israel (34:9; 35:6); lair of jackals for Edom, plots of reeds for Israel (34:13; 35:7). Many of these penalties had already been promised for Babylon in chapter 13, but the clarity of the contrast reaches its zenith in these two chapters.

4 Sennacherib threatens Jerusalem (1)

Isaiah 36:1—37:8

Both Isaiah and the historical account of 2 Kings (18:13—19:8 and 19:9–37) contain two versions of Sennacherib's invasion. The account in the Assyrian records confirm the historical outline with the report that in 701BC Sennacherib besieged 46 cities of Judah, capturing or destroying them and leaving Hezekiah in Jerusalem 'shut up like a bird in a cage'.

This first vivid description of the embassy of the Rabshakeh, the high-ranking envoy of Sennacherib, who himself was busy besieging Lachish in the coastal plain, as a preliminary to marching on Jerusalem itself, is brilliantly presented. He gives Jerusalem a final chance to avoid the horrors of siege. To begin with, ironically the dialogue takes place at exactly the same place where King Ahaz had, a few years before, refused Isaiah's offer (with his significantly-named son, 'A-Remnant-Will-Return') of a sign from the Lord, presented in Isaiah 7:1–17.

Second, the Rabshakeh deliberately avoids the diplomatic language of Aramaic in favour of the local Hebrew dialect to ensure that all the people, hanging over the walls, understand what he says. Then he points out that Egypt (Jerusalem's chosen ally) is a sharp and broken reed, that the king has openly submitted his God to their gods by accepting an Assyrian-style altar, and that the king could not even supply cavalrymen if presented with horses for them to ride. The most audacious rhetoric of all is his rosy picture – surely with his tongue in his cheek – of the delights of exile to Babylon. Just take a look at the Lachish sculptures in the British Museum of captives slaving away at building-work!

We are left with two puzzling elements, which fail to fit in entirely. This account does not mention the snippet from the parallel account in 2 Kings 18:14–16, that Hezekiah had already at some stage paid a heavy tribute to Sennacherib, which obliged him not only to accept an altar of pagan (and so unclean) design, but even to strip off the gold from the doors of the temple. Does Hezekiah still possess enough treasure to pay a significant bribe to keep Sennacherib away? In addition there is the strange story in the Greek historian Herodotus (2:141) that Sennacherib withdrew from his attack on Egypt because of a plague of rodents which gnawed through their bow-strings; could this be a garbled account that an attack of bubonic plague left them helpless, so that they were compelled to withdraw?

5 Sennacherib threatens Jerusalem (2)

Isaiah 37:9–38

The second version of Sennacherib's threats omits the drama of the Rabshakeh's bragging speech to concentrate on the piety of Hezekiah and the mockery and insult offered by Sennacherib to 'the Holy One of Israel'. The contrast between the self-confidence of the Rabshakeh, and of the boast put in Sennacherib's mouth (vv. 24–25) and the humility of Hezekiah is marked. The Lord's final reaction is to put a hook through Sennacherib's nostrils and a bit on his lips. The account concludes with what is virtually a fulfilment of this threat: Sennacherib's death at the hands of his own sons in his own temple. This is confirmed by Assyrian records; it occurred some 20 years later.

It is worth saying a word about this special this title, 'the Holy One of Israel'. It pervades especially the book of Isaiah, being used affectionately by Isaiah more than 25 times, from the initial vocation-vision of Isaiah in 6:3, in the second part of Isaiah 43:3, 14 and the third, post-exilic prophecies (60:14). Elsewhere it occurs only four times in the Psalms and twice elsewhere in the Hebrew Bible. It implies that the holiness of the Lord somehow creates a special bond with Israel and belongs especially to Israel: 'Cry aloud and shout for joy, you who live in Zion, for great in your midst is the Holy One of Israel' (Isaiah 12:6), or 'Your redeemer is the Holy One of Israel' (41:14). The Hebrew word for 'holy' (*qadosh*) means basically 'weight' and 'dignity'. There is about it an awed reverence and an affectionate untouchability. It is important to wash before and after contact with something holy. This is why Jesus tells the cured man born blind to wash in the cleansing Pool of Siloam (John 9:11).

Two favourite passages give a feeling for this concept: when the law is to be given on Mount Sinai, the Israelites are afraid to set foot on the mountain for fear of its holiness. When Israel is passing through the desert, the ark of the covenant, in which the Lord resides, is too holy to be stationed within the camp for fear of contamination. Or again, when Moses goes out to converse with the Lord in the tent of meeting all the elders stand at the entrance to their tents, bowed in reverence as he passes.

6 The sickness and recovery of Hezekiah

Isaiah 38

This story of Hezekiah's sickness and recovery occurs also in 2 Kings 20:1–11 with minor variations. Here it is inserted independently, with only a vague time-reference. It is an important instance of the Lord withdrawing from his sentence, even after it has been pronounced, at the evidence of prayer and repentance. It is placed here to contrast sharply with the death of Sennacherib, the persecutor of Israel immediately preceding it, stressing the fidelity and prayerfulness of Hezekiah. In this account Hezekiah does not ask for a sign, as he does in the version of 2 Kings. In this again there is a contrast with King Ahaz, who refused to ask for a sign. The extra 15 years of life are offered spontaneously by the prophet (v. 6), making Hezekiah's final comment superfluous and rather clumsy. His recovery is also a symbol of the recovery of Jerusalem from its destruction and from the exile itself.

Hezekiah's lovely psalm-like prayer of thanksgiving (which does not occur in the version of 2 Kings) has no intrinsic connection with his illness and is surely inserted independently. The book of Proverbs 25:1 notes that there was literary activity at the court of King Hezekiah. The psalm has three striking images of endings (the vanished shepherd's tent, the weaver and the loom), then three lively images of animals (the lion, the swallow and the dove), then three grim images of horrors avoided (Sheol, death and the pit) to sum up God's care of his devoted servant.

Guidelines

This week's readings from Isaiah take us into the world of the end of the Babylonian domination of the Near East, when the city of Babylon was about to be conquered by Cyrus in 538BC. The period is introduced by a threatening poem on the fall of Babylon, followed by a satire mocking the pretensions of the King of Babylon himself. Then follows in the book of Isaiah a series of poems on the disasters destined for the small states in their unsuccessful struggle to fend off the mighty forces of the Mesopotamian powers during the previous decades, the Philistines, Moab, Damascus, Egypt, Tyre and others. These do not all stem from the prophet Isaiah personally, but are spread over the period of two centuries, emphasizing the detailed control of the Lord over the whole of world history. This is especially valid for the later prophecies which border on the apocalyptic. The Lord will continue to guard his people of Israel through all the changes and crises of history.

Questions:

- How do you imagine the end of the world?
- Does hell exist? In what sense?
- Is there anyone in hell? Could we help that person?
- Is God merciful? In what way?
- Are the Jews still the people of God?

FURTHER READING

Joseph Blenkinsopp, *Isaiah 1—39*, *Isaiah 40—55* and *Isaiah 56—66 (Anchor Yale Bible Commentaries)* (Bantam, 2000, 2002, 2003)

John D. W. Watts, *Isaiah 1—33* and *Isaiah 34—66 (Word Biblical Commentary)* (Thomas Nelson, 2005, revised editions)

Theology of mental health

Rachel Newham

Mental health is being spoken about more now than ever. We have awareness weeks, campaigns and courses designed to enable us to see our health as more than physical, to try to dismantle the stigma around mental illness that sees people called 'crazy' or 'schizo' when they're struggling.

And yet when we look for it, we see that scripture has been talking about mental health and addressing the lack of support for it for millennia. The creation narratives offer us a vision of what positive mental health can look like, and throughout the biblical story, we see people experience and struggle with their emotions; whether that be the despair that David describes in so many of his psalms, how the community of Israel dealt with their homesickness in exile or how Jesus himself wrestled with his emotions.

The beauty of the way the Bible approaches mental health is that it not only demonstrates the way creation is set up to aid mental health (Genesis 2) but also recognises the importance of our emotions by giving us models of how to bring them to God in lament while holding on to the hope that is to come.

Not only that, but Jesus brings new hope for life lived to the fullest and draws us to the ultimate hope we have in a recreated world where we have redeemed hearts, bodies and minds.

These readings are a journey through how our minds and hearts are meant to flourish, how far they've fallen, but also the hope we have in what is to come, so I pray that we can see how scripture not only supports our mental health but meets us when health feels like a distant dream.

Consider reading these passages and/or notes in the company of others. I always discover new insights, even when I've read the passages countless times before. I pray that you glimpse something of God's *shalom* and hope for us as you read.

Bible quotations are taken from the NIV.

1 *Shalom*

Genesis 2:1–9, 15–29

The creation narratives are often overly familiar to us, so I invite you to read with new eyes. Look for what it says about how God created us and the world we live in, with conditions that allowed us to flourish, but also what it can tell us about how to live well in these fallen, sometimes dark days.

As you read, consider how the elements of *shalom*, which is often simply translated as 'peace', is far richer and more nuanced, and the word which probably comes closest to our contemporary understanding of mental health. *Shalom* means wholeness in body, mind and soul, but it extends beyond individual mental health; it also includes how communities can function at their best with everything working together towards flourishing.

God rested on the seventh day, and it's a reminder that God did not rest from the work of creating because he was tired (for God is inexhaustible), but because it is what is right for humanity, and he's modelling that.

We cannot have anything close to full *shalom*, wholeness in our mental health, without a rhythm of rest that restores us. The work we are called to do is to be from a place of rest, rather than us resting just because we are exhausted and have no choice. This rhythm is easier when we think of sabbath as the start of our week, as our Jewish friends do, rather than something we limp towards after our work is completed.

We also see all the elements for positive mental well-being set before us; from the 'trees that are pleasing to the eye and good for food' (v. 9) which represent our need not just for nourishment but for beauty, to the importance of relationships – not just through Adam and Eve but as a reflection of the triune God, and the way they walk through Eden free from shame.

It's also important to remember that work and purpose were part of our needs from the very beginning. Work isn't merely the result of the fall – we were made to take part in God's creative endeavour. *Shalom* is not just related to paid work, but anything that contributes to the world.

The story of creation shows us that we matter because we were crafted by the King, with purpose and love, to be a part of the world for his pleasure. It is due to the King's love and our God-given purpose that we can have *shalom* and know we are loved.

2 Homesick

Jeremiah 29:4–14

The hardest thing to reconcile is how quickly the glimpse of *shalom*, which Genesis shows us, falls apart. Adam and Eve are exiled from paradise, where all their needs were met, but in a sign of his great mercy, their shame is clothed even as they learn to live outside of Eden.

It's a story of mercy which follows exiled people, and while it doesn't remove the ache of homesickness, it provides a memory of wholeness that plants the seed of hope.

God's people spend generation after generation seeking, finding and losing their home – and the grief of this experience is echoed in the struggles people have with their mental health. The grief, loneliness and isolation that mental illness engenders is seen echoed as God's people cry out to him, first from Egypt, then from Babylon.

In both cases, we see that the goodness God has shown is swiftly forgotten in the face of present pain, and isn't that the same for us too?

Jeremiah 29 is a famous text which adorned anything from magnets and mugs in the 90s, but we often miss that this is a letter to those in exile, and it offers great wisdom and encouragement for us when we are going through our own feelings of homesickness for what life might have been like before mental health struggles arose.

There is an acknowledgement of the Israelites' situation, but there is no dismissal of it. God does not declare that no good can be done in the pain of the loss. Instead, we see an encouragement to build a life anyway.

This can often seem impossible in the face of health stripped away, but we cannot spend our times of struggle simply wishing it away. In the face of their exile, Jeremiah commands them to 'build houses and settle down; plant gardens and eat what they produce' (v. 5). For us, this might be using the little energy we possess to keep a single hobby going, or it might be taking the help that is offered, even when we have little hope it will actually help.

It seems that much of the experience of exile, then and now, relies on us allowing others to hold our hope for us until we can reclaim it for ourselves, trusting that just as he did for the exiles, God will fulfil his promises.

3 Lament

Psalm 88

Psalm 88 is unique in many ways. It is relentless in its complaint and unlike other psalms of lament, it contains no resolution. There is no turning point at which the psalmist finds comfort in an element God's character or by remembering a past victory.

And yet that is precisely why it reflects the spiritual nature of mental health struggles so accurately. For, amid mental anguish, there is often an inability to rationalise or orient yourself to God. This may be because of destructive thought patterns, fatigue or unrelenting hopelessness. It can feel as if past victories were a fluke, or that your best days are behind you.

The hope in this psalm, however, is its very inclusion in the Bible. A text that ends with such stark bleakness, 'surely darkness is my closest friend' (v. 14) is not deemed unacceptable to God or outside of his loving care.

Lament is woven throughout scripture and, put simply, is the practice of bringing what hurts to God. But what makes it an act of faith is that these words are not just uttered into the ether, but addressed to the Creator of the universe. As theologian J. Todd Billings (who himself lives with incurable cancer) writes, 'We only fully enter lament when we realise that we're not just expressing ourselves to a human observer but bringing our burdens before the Lord, the Creator, the Almighty who – in light of our distress – is our Deliverer' (see Billings, *Rejoicing in Lament*).

Despite the lack of resolution and the absence of words of rescue or hope, the writer of Psalm 88 and those who faithfully compiled the Bible show us that we can bring whatever darkness we face and need not hide these feelings from our heavenly Father.

Sometimes prayers like this one may result in deliverance from a painful situation. Still, in every situation, we can be assured that we will not be left to face the darkness alone, because voicing our hopelessness invites the God of all hope to be with us.

4 Weeping

John 11:17–37

Perhaps what speaks most to me about how God cares for our mental health is that when he sent Jesus, he was not an emotionless automaton, but experienced the whole spectrum of human emotions in glorious, multi-coloured display.

He relaxed over meals with his close friends, got angered by injustice, was moved with compassion, wept in grief and was overwhelmed 'to the point of death' (Matthew 26:38) on the night before his crucifixion. He was not just a physical being, but an emotional one.

It is a demonstration to me that our emotions are not inherently sinful – they may drive sinful behaviour, for example, by lashing out at someone when we get angry – but it's not the anger that's the problem, but how we manage that anger. For instance, Jesus was without sin and yet exhibited anger powerfully when driving out the sellers in the temple.

Jesus' friendship with Mary, Martha and Lazarus puts his emotional life on full display. Despite knowing (presumably) the miracle he is about to perform, Jesus comforts the grieving sisters with compassion, which can mean 'to suffer with', and this willingness to suffer is a hallmark of his love both for his friends and for the whole of humanity.

We read that Jesus was 'deeply moved in spirit and troubled' (v. 33) and in the words of the shortest verse of the Bible that 'Jesus wept' (v. 35). The weeping is taken not just a sign of grief, but of love – a reminder perhaps that the two are inextricably linked.

Jesus' move to comfort the mourning sisters, as well as expressing his own grief, is a permission slip if we needed one that our emotions, even those that feel painful, are made in the image of God.

There is no need to have a stiff upper lip approach to our mental health – we are as free to express it to one another as we are to offer it to God in lament. As Paul wrote in 2 Corinthians 1:4, we receive the comfort of God, and we are to offer it to one another with honesty and hope.

Our weeping will be comforted by the living God, and we are to share that comfort, cultivating communities that do not expect a faith built on 'stiff upper lips' but ones that welcome and include our emotions as part of what it means to be human.

5 Presence

John 14:15–31

The end of Jesus' earthly ministry does not signal an end to God's active care for our mental health and emotions; the Spirit that once hovered over the waters at creation is sent to be *paraclete*, a helper in times of trouble and an advocate, who will remain close even when Jesus no longer walks the earth.

This is the Holy Spirit, sent at Pentecost to continue the ever-presence of the Lord with his people, fulfilling Jesus' promise as he delivered the great commission that he will be with us 'always, to the very end of the age' (Matthew 28:20). Here we are not promised a life free from trouble, but we are assured that his peace will remain with us.

At the heart of so many mental health struggles lies a deep anxiety and loneliness; these emotions often go beyond words and feel impossible to communicate with those around us and with God.

It is into this pain that we are assured and comforted that the Spirit meets us.

Paul writes in his letter to the Romans that: 'In the same way, the Spirit helps us in our weakness. We do not know what we ought to pray for, but the Spirit himself intercedes for us through wordless groans' (8:26).

Being able to communicate our pain, even when we don't have a language for it, is a powerful gift spiritually and psychologically. It follows the old maxim 'a problem shared is a problem halved' which, while not mathematically true, is reflected in what we know psychologically that talking about our difficulties can reduce our stress and distress.

The gift of the Holy Spirit is the gift of God's presence with us. For when pain fills the horizon and we don't have language for it, God's Spirit is with us. This is no offer of a prosperity-style gospel which promises an end to pain, but the comforter who translates our wordless agonies into prayers seeking the ceaseless care of the Creator.

6 Hope of home

Revelation 21:1–8

It's often easy to shrink our hope to something almost fanciful; angels gliding around on clouds while singing endlessly, or perhaps an eternal church service (which may or may not delight you!).

And yet the reality of the hope we have in Jesus goes beyond our polemic of fluffy heaven and fiery hell. We are instead offered the vision of a recreated, redeemed heaven and earth where we will once more walk in step with our Creator, never again to question his existence or character, but held evermore in his love.

As theologian Tom Wright helpfully explains: 'the ultimate destination is… not "going to heaven when you die" but being bodily raised into the transformed glorious likeness of Jesus' (*Surprised by Hope*, SPCK, 2005).

In some ways, the sheer unimaginability of it is comforting; there will be no echo of the pains of this life, and we cannot begin to comprehend what a recreated heaven and earth will look like. We can be sure of nothing except that we will be with our Lord.

The pain and questions that torture us here will pass away in the presence of God's glory, which will be so bright it leaves no shadow or darkness in its wake.

Perhaps the most comforting element of this held but known future hope, for those who struggle with their mental health is written in Revelation 21:4: 'He will wipe every tear from their eyes… There will be no more death, or mourning, or crying or pain.' It was certainly the hope that I clung to most fiercely when I first began to grapple with poor mental health in my teenage years and it seemed as though my tears would never cease.

In the grand cosmic design for recreation, we still have a Lord and Saviour who cares for our tears with the gentleness of a parent who wipes their children's eyes of the pains of the day and the night.

Hope, in the unseen and unknown future of the world, can be trusted because we know that the Jesus who wept, comforted and cared for those around him reigns on the throne forevermore.

Guidelines

Sometimes, reading familiar scriptures through a new lens can feel uncomfortable, like putting on a new pair of glasses and finding yourself adjusting to your new view. I hope that as we've journeyed through the passages together, you've been able to gain insights that you'd not noticed before, that you've seen the vision both for what the fullness of mental wellbeing can be (and what we can hope for), but also how we are met in our painful times by the mercy and kindness of God.

God has given humanity a whole range of emotions, from the deepest joys to the most wretched grief, but also a way to communicate those often-wordless emotions to him through the Spirit and by offering ourselves up with lament.

Allow yourself to ask questions in your prayer times about the purpose of different emotions and how you can be a better steward of your own feelings and those expressed to you.

How might having a vision of the fullness of *shalom*, as shown in Genesis 2, impact how we approach our own mental health and that of those we're responsible for? Are there practices we might put in place to help us promote and protect our mental health, for example, by making sure we carve out a rest day each week to practice sabbath (for clergy or parents this might not be a Sunday, but a time you can protect each week to spend resting and reconnecting with God).

Think about how you spend your time with God at the moment. Do you have times of gratitude as well as times of grief? If the idea of lament feels alien to you, consider using the liturgical year to give yourself some structure: as a starting point, use Advent and Lent to quiet chaotic souls and bring all that is painful in your life and the world around you to God. You might wish to follow the Carmelite themes of Advent (waiting, accepting, journeying and birthing) to guide you.

Pick one of your favourite Bible stories and go through it, highlighting each emotion that is described, considering if the emotions were expressed helpfully or destructively. Offer each emotion in prayer, considering what the function of the feeling is and asking God to show you how you can use these emotions for his glory.

FURTHER READING

Dan Allender and Tremper Longman, *The Cry of the Soul: How our emotions reveal our deepest questions about God* (The Navigators, 2015).

J. Todd Billings, *Rejoicing in Lament: Wrestling with incurable cancer and life in Christ* (Brazos Press, 2016).

Pete Greig, *God on Mute: Engaging the silence of unanswered prayer* (Baker Publishing Group, 2011).

Sharon Hastings, *Tending to My Thoughts: A doctor with severe mental illness finds recovery* (IVP, 2024).

Isabelle Hamley and Chris Cook (eds), *The Bible and Mental Health: Towards a biblical theology of mental health* (SCM Press, 2020).

Rachael Newham, *Learning to Breathe: My journey with mental illness* (SPCK, 2018).

Patrick Regan, *Honesty Over Silence: It's OK not to be OK* (SPCK, 2024).

Peter Scazzero, *Emotionally Healthy Spirituality* (Zondervan, 2017).

John Swinton, *Finding Jesus in the Storm: The spiritual lives of Christians with mental health challenges* (William. B. Eerdmans, 2020).

Malachi: the six disputes

Olivia Warburton

The last book in the Old Testament, Malachi can be dated to around the time when Ezra and then Nehemiah came to Jerusalem, 80 to 90 years after the Israelites began to return from exile in Babylon in 538BC. The prophets Haggai and Zechariah were writing at roughly the same time, and Malachi is located immediately after their books to become the final book of the twelve minor prophets.

Sacrifices have recommenced and the Second Temple has been rebuilt (515BC), but all is not well. Malachi calls for spiritual reformation.

Reading the book of Malachi is like listening in on a heated Q&A session between God and the people of Israel. Across four chapters, there are six disputes or arguments. The general pattern is that God makes a statement, the people disagree with it or question it, and God then responds to their challenge. Nobody pulls their punches; there's plenty of rhetoric, accusation and sarcasm.

What are they arguing about? God condemns the Israelites' apathy and corruption, while at the same time seeking to convince them how much they are loved. There are references to a future time of judgement, refining and deliverance. Direct quotations from Malachi, together with a number of plausible echoes, appear across the New Testament, and we will look at the most significant of these.

The book's authorship is not clearly established. Since the word *malachi* means 'my messenger' or 'my angel', it may well be a title or nickname rather than the prophet's actual name. It has been suggested that the author was a Levite (some say Ezra himself), and if this is the case it adds a poignant personal dimension to the prophet's harsh words against the priesthood in the first two chapters of the book.

Bible quotations are taken from the NIV.

1 Do you really love me?

Malachi 1:1–5

Reading this first exchange between God and the people of Israel is like coming in halfway through a lovers' tiff or a stand-off between parent and child. God's 'I have loved you' (v. 2) does not convince them and they ask for proof. It's no surprise that the traumatic experience of exile in Babylon and the far-from-problem-free return to Jerusalem appear to have left the Israelites seriously doubting God's faithfulness and good purposes. Despite the restoration, how could a loving God have let these things happen to them in the first place? It's a question we would probably all ask – and do ask, when times are tough.

God's response is essentially, 'You've always been the only one for me,' reminding them how far back this goes by referencing how their ancestor Jacob was chosen to bear God's covenant promises through the generations (see Genesis 25—28). Jacob's older twin Esau (Edom) was not chosen, and this is the meaning of 'hate', as opposed to a visceral emotion of dislike. As we see in Obadiah, Edom came to ruin, but the Israelites have been loved and brought back to their promised land.

In Romans 9:13, Paul quotes Malachi 1:2–3 in support of God's sovereign, unknowable decision-making. He continues, 'What then shall we say? Is God unjust? Not at all! For he says to Moses, "I will have mercy on whom I have mercy, and I will have compassion on whom I have compassion"' (vv. 14–15).

As descendants of Jacob, the ancient people of Israel were, and continued to be, blessed by God as God's chosen people. Indeed, God's reference back to the covenant made with Jacob should have reminded the Israelites of this promise, made to their forefather but so relevant to their current situation: 'I am with you and will watch over you wherever you go, and I will bring you back to this land. I will not leave you until I have done what I have promised you' (Genesis 28:15).

To those Israelites who believed that God could or would only work in their own land, verse 5 offers a corrective. In fact, the Lord is great 'even beyond the borders of Israel!'

2 We haven't done anything wrong

Malachi 1:6—2:9

The second dispute is longer and more drawn out. Here the priests are under fire. God tells them, 'It is you priests who show contempt for my name,' and they retaliate by asking how they are supposed to have done this (1:6). In chapters 2 and 3 we see covenant relationships broken in different ways: through divorce, through injustice, through withholding tithes. Here the covenant between God and the people is damaged because the priests are 'offering defiled food on my altar' (1:7). The people are short-changing God by offering sacrifices of sick, blemished animals, and the priests are complicit in this.

Frustrated, God gives examples of how the relationship should work – as a son honours his father, or a slave respects his master (1:6) – and asks, would you treat your governor this way (v. 8)? In fact, God is a great king, to be feared among the nations (1:14)! It's also clear from verse 14 that the people's behaviour is a matter of choice, not necessity: other, better animals are available but are deliberately being withheld. Echoes back to Cain (Genesis 4:3–5) and forward to Ananias and Sapphira (Acts 5:1–2) can be heard.

It's a failure to honour God, and it's also a sign of flawed leadership. The people are cutting corners with their sacrifices and the priests are letting them, with no attempt at rebuke or discipleship. As leaders, they will most definitely be held accountable.

God rejects these worship offerings, which are anything but, and the indictment continues in chapter 2. The priests' blessings are already cursed (2:2), they are already dishonoured before the people (2:9), and worse is to come if they do not change their ways (2:3). Covenant language is explicit: the priests have violated the covenant with Levi (2:8), 'who revered me and stood in awe of my name' (2:5). Levi is the archetype of their calling; the role model they should follow: 'True instruction was in his mouth and nothing false was found on his lips' (2:6).

It appears that the shoddy sacrifices are not the only problem: 'The lips of a priest ought to preserve knowledge... But you have turned from the way and by your teaching have caused many to stumble' (2:7–8). They have also 'shown partiality in matters of the law' (2:9). In matters of worship, teaching and social justice, they have comprehensively fallen short.

3 I'll do what I want

Malachi 2:10–16

In the third dispute, it's the turn of the Israelite men to answer for their behaviour, although here, unusually, God does all the talking and there is no comeback. God first condemns marrying 'women who worship a foreign god' (v. 11). Presumably the women's example is drawing their husbands away from the God of Israel and they are adopting the worship of their wives' ancestral gods, with religious and cultural knock-on effects for the whole family. Nehemiah 13:23–24 states that 'half of their children… did not know how to speak the language of Judah'.

But then the focus shifts, perhaps unexpectedly, to an injunction to husbands not to divorce their wives. Indeed, God makes it clear that their offerings are being rejected specifically because of their unfaithfulness to the marriage covenant (v. 14). God is against the practice of divorce, whether this takes the form of setting aside Jewish wives in order to take foreign wives or foreign wives in order to take Jewish wives.

The Hebrew of verse 16 is ambiguous, with some translations rendering it as 'I hate divorce'. This has at times been taken out of context to discourage wives from leaving abusive husbands (see Helen Paynter, *The Bible Doesn't Tell Me So*, BRF Ministries, 2020). But the message is clear enough. It's a message to the man – who in that society was the only partner with the ability to initiate divorce – that God is watching. It's about not making an existing power imbalance far, far worse.

Divorce could be catastrophic for women. If they didn't have a father or brother to take them back when the marriage ended, it left them financially unprotected and personally vulnerable to every kind of abuse. Three times in verses 14–16 the men are accused of faithlessness, using a word (*bagad*) whose root meaning is to behave treacherously, to break a covenant. And this breach of covenant is described in terms of violence (*hamas*) against the wife: '"The man who hates and divorces his wife," says the Lord, the God of Israel, "does violence to the one he should protect"' (v. 16).

In the next chapter, we see again God's heart for the vulnerable and marginalised in the warning to those 'who oppress the widows and the fatherless, and deprive the foreigners among you of justice, but do not fear me' (3:5).

4 What's the point?

Malachi 2:17—3:5

In the fourth dispute, the Israelites have found their voices again. They cite the prevalence of evil and injustice and complain that God is doing nothing about it, saying, 'Where is the God of justice?' (2:17). It's a complaint that surfaces frequently in the biblical narrative (see for example Psalm 94), but here God is 'wearied' by it, doubtless because of the implied slur on the divine character: 'All who do evil are good in the eyes of the Lord, and he is pleased with them.'

God responds by promising action: 'Then suddenly the Lord you are seeking will come to his temple; the messenger of the covenant, whom you desire, will come' (3:1). The word *malachi* is used again to denote 'messenger'. This messenger will 'prepare the way before me' and is interpreted in the New Testament as referring to John the Baptist preparing the way for Jesus (see Matthew 11:10; Mark 1:2; Luke 7:27).

God's intervention, however, may not be exactly what the people have in mind: 'But who can endure the day of his coming? Who can stand when he appears?' (3:2). It will be 'sudden' (in the sense that a catastrophe is sudden) and will come like a fire to purify the people and restore righteousness. The failures of the priesthood are pointedly revisited: the messenger will 'purify the Levites and refine them like gold and silver. Then the Lord will have men who will bring offerings in righteousness, and the offerings of Judah and Jerusalem will be acceptable to the Lord, as in days gone by' (3:3–4).

In response to the people's accusation that God does not care about social injustice, God promises to prosecute a trial in which all perpetrators will be held to account (3:5).

There is an interesting echo of the language of 3:3 in 1 Peter 1:6–7, which recasts Malachi's brilliant yet intimidating vision of the 'day of his coming' into a more encouraging message for faithful believers: 'In all this you greatly rejoice, though now for a little while you may have had to suffer grief in all kinds of trials. These have come so that the proven genuineness of your faith – of greater worth than gold, which perishes even though refined by fire – may result in praise, glory and honour when Jesus Christ is revealed.'

5 So tell us what to do

Malachi 3:6–12

In the fifth dispute, God calls the people to 'return to me, and I will return to you' (v. 7). In what is by now a standard response, they ask for clarification (not once, but twice, as in 1:6–7). The answer is very simple and very practical, leaving them nowhere to hide. God reminds them that they are no longer offering a tithe of their income to the temple: 'Bring the whole tithe into the storehouse, that there may be food in my house' (v. 10).

Tithing to support the temple was legislated in Leviticus 27:30: 'A tithe of everything from the land, whether grain from the soil or fruit from the trees, belongs to the Lord.' Yet it is clear from Nehemiah 13:10–13 that this had ceased to happen. God is anxious to bless the people – which includes blessing the land (v. 11) – if they will only be wholehearted in their commitment. The short-changing of the tithe mirrors the short-changing of the sacrifices in chapter 1.

God issues a remarkable challenge, which is not found anywhere else in the Bible: 'Test me in this… and see if I will not fling open the floodgates of heaven' (v. 10). As a general rule, the biblical narrative indicates that God should not be put to the test. Ahaz is invited to ask for a sign in Isaiah 7:11, and 1 John 4:1 speaks of the importance of testing the spirits to see whether they are from God, but Gideon's double fleece experiment in Judges 6:36–40 is more suggestive of a lack of faith, and Jesus routs the devil in the wilderness (Matthew 4:7) by quoting Deuteronomy 6:16.

Here, however, God is eager to be put to the test. If the people can only bring themselves to act in generous surrender to their God, unstoppable streams of mercy and blessing will flow. With more of everything, more can be given – a virtuous circle. In Luke 6:38, Jesus repeats this challenge: 'Give, and it will be given to you. A good measure, pressed down, shaken together and running over, will be poured into your lap. For with the measure you use, it will be measured to you.'

6 What's the point (again)?

Malachi 3:13—4:6

In the sixth and final dispute, the people claim that it is pointless to serve God, building on their accusation in Malachi 2:17. God now describes this attitude as arrogance (3:13). All they can see is that 'evildoers prosper, and even when they put God to the test, they get away with it' (3:14), while apparently ignoring the radical encouragement in the previous section to test God themselves.

The scene shifts to the faithful remnant, who make their appearance for the first time (3:16). As Elijah found to his surprise in 1 Kings 19:18, there are some who remain faithful – it's not all doom and gloom! A scroll of remembrance is created by this 'treasured possession', with God's language of the relationship between father and son (3:17) recalling 1:6 and pointing forward to 4:6.

In the conclusion to the book, 4:1–3 develops the imagery of the 'day of his coming' from the previous chapter. There is a warning not only for evildoers but for the arrogant, whom the people need to recognise as themselves (see 3:13–14). The faithful remnant, however, need not fear this day of purifying judgement: instead of a furnace, the fire will be like the rays of the rising sun, bringing life and healing.

The final three verses of Malachi reference both Moses and Elijah, and through them the Torah and the Prophets. The listener, or reader, is first called to 'remember the law of my servant Moses, the decrees and laws I gave him at Horeb for all Israel' (4:4). There is then the promise to send the prophet Elijah (4:5–6) – a prophecy which is explicitly linked in the gospels to John the Baptist, where the angel says to Zechariah, 'He will go on before the Lord, in the spirit and power of Elijah, to turn the hearts of the parents to their children and the disobedient to the wisdom of the righteous – to make ready a people prepared for the Lord' (Luke 1:17).

Perched at the very end of the Old Testament, Malachi points firmly forward to the New, where true restoration of relationships – between parent and child, slave and master, husband and wife, and Jew and Gentile – can begin to happen when the Son of Righteousness is revealed.

Guidelines

Peter Adam's *The Message of Malachi* notes that 'a striking feature of the book is the way in which every word of God is contradicted or questioned by his people'. Many commentators view this in an entirely negative light. Whether some of the back-and-forth could be more favourably interpreted as robust engagement, wrestling with God in the style of Abraham, Jacob or the psalm writers, is for you to decide!

Look back through the six disputes and pray through the areas of Christian discipleship that emerge. Which themes resonate most with you?

- Malachi 1:2–5: Believing that God loves us and wants the best for us
- Malachi 1:6—2:9: Faithful, uncompromised leadership
- Malachi 2:10–16: Commitment and integrity in personal relationships
- Malachi 2:17—3:5: God's heart for social justice
- Malachi 3:6–12: Trusting God with our resources
- Malachi 3:13—4:6: Trusting that God sees the bigger picture

---

FURTHER READING

Peter Adam, *The Message of Malachi (The Bible Speaks Today Old Testament Commentary)* (IVP, 2024).

Grace Emmerson, *Nahum to Malachi (The People's Bible Commentary)* (BRF Ministries, 1998).

Julia M. O'Brien, *The Oxford Handbook of the Minor Prophets (Oxford Handbooks)* (OUP USA, 2021).

Grace in the New Testament

David Spriggs

'Let us say the grace together': words so often uttered at the end of a service, with the closing words (or similar): 'The grace of the Lord Jesus Christ, and the love of God, and the fellowship of the Holy Spirit, be with you all' (see 2 Corinthians 13:13).

Most of the congregation know them off by heart, but frequency dulls the senses, and how many know where they come from?

Sometimes we may be called on to 'say grace', perhaps at a church tea, a wedding banquet or even a formal civic meal. On these occasions we don't say 'the grace' but offer a prayer of thanks for the meal we are going to share together.

'Grace' might also be a TV detective, your daughter's name or even your own, in which case the word will bring to mind a person with a history and a physical image.

But within the New Testament, grace is so much richer than any of these. It takes us to the core truths of our faith, on which all Christian community is based and from which all compassion and mission must flow. It can be considered as one of our core values; a USP for the church. Understood properly, it triggers an overwhelming sense of gratitude for all that we have received, as well as all that we will. Above all, it prompts an association with a unique historical person who has eternal significance – Jesus Christ our Lord. Many of Paul's writings are an exploration, celebration and defence of grace, but other New Testament writers also affirm the centrality of this divine reality.

While such a key word has many connotations, it is above all the identity of grace with Jesus which is astounding. Expect to have your mind challenged and your heart enlivened!

Bible quotations are taken from the NRSV.

1 Grace is Jesus

John 1:10–18

On three occasions in this short and theologically rich passage, we find John's gospel focusing on grace. John identifies the reality of grace with first 'the Word' and then Jesus. Twice within a few verses we find the phrase 'grace and truth'. The very first time Jesus is named in the Prologue is with the statement 'grace and truth came through Jesus Christ' (v. 17). John brings the Word into both historical context (John the Baptist in verse 6; see also vv. 10–13) and theological focus. The Word becomes light and then flesh, with the 'glory as of a father's only son' (v. 14). Now Jesus is revealed as 'full of grace and truth'! Commentators note the similarity to the Hebrew pair 'loyalty [grace] and truth' as markers of God's character. But there is also a difference, as the Hebrew 'grace' is normally translated 'mercy' in the original Septuagint. While we shall see that grace includes mercy, it is far deeper and more extensive.

The second time that the phrase 'grace and truth' occurs, it distinguishes the old covenant from the new: 'The law indeed was given through Moses; grace and truth came through Jesus Christ' (v. 17). This underlines the significance of Jesus as at least on a par with Moses, and elevates him as the one who inaugurates the new covenant. In these few words contrasting the law and 'grace and truth', the real nature of Jesus and his superiority to the very best of Israel's faith is underlined.

John emphasises too that this 'grace and truth' is in no way a diminishing of or a deviation from the reality of the Old Covenant: 'We have seen his glory, the glory as of a father's only son' (v. 14). God's glory is the manifestation of his real nature. In projecting 'grace and truth', Jesus is revealing to us the inner nature of God the Father.

Another important strand is that Jesus is 'full' of grace and truth, and this fullness is the source of our experience and transformation by encounter with Jesus: 'From his fullness we have all received, grace upon grace' (v. 16).

C.K. Barrett points out that this indicates that 'Christian life is based at all points on grace…one grace is exchanged only for another' (Barrett, p.140).

2 Grace abounding

Ephesians 1:3–14

This passage helps us get a more precise feel for the texture of grace. In verse 6, Paul writes of '[God's] glorious grace', and in the next verse 'the riches of his grace that he lavished upon us'.

In the light of these descriptors – glorious, riches, lavished on us – it has been rightly said, 'There is a certain inexhaustible abundance in the grace of God… there is a certain infinity; a certain complete adequacy; a certain inexhaustibility and illimitableness' (Barclay, p. 123).

The secular image of lavishing riches on someone includes a despot showing favour to a subject, perhaps because of a woman's beauty or some loyal service rendered. But the emphasis is on the almost inexplicable generosity of the giver, rather than the attributes of the person being so favoured.

Grace is 'glorious' because it, as it were, glistens and shines and glimmers. There is nothing ordinary or mundane about God's grace. It is 'riches': it has nothing mean or measured about it, and it never runs out. It is 'lavished upon us': in no way does God calculate the least amount he can get away with; exactly the opposite, he pours it on us like perfume until we are almost overwhelmed by it. It recalls the feast in Psalm 23:5: 'You prepare a table before me in the presence of my enemies… my cup overflows.'

An even stronger image is that of the excited, spontaneous but intentional generosity of the father in Luke 15:11–32 when his son returns home. Ephesians 1:6 reinforces this texture: 'To the praise of his glorious grace that he freely bestowed on us in the Beloved.' It is given absolutely freely.

Such unbelievable generosity inevitably sparks a response in the recipients, being so overwhelmed by the experience that they can only respond in praise. It draws us away from ourselves, even our experience of such generosity, and releases in us thanksgiving and a desire to honour the one whose 'favour' has transformed us.

3 Grace: beginning and end

Romans 1:7; 16:20

One of the standout characteristics of Paul's letters is that he always begins and ends with a salutation which involves grace. This is true when he is writing to a church he founded and knows well, and equally when he writes to Rome. It is as true of the main Pauline corpus as of those some scholars question (e.g. Ephesians and Colossians). It applies when he is being affirming (e.g. Philippians) but also when he is at his most challenging and critical (e.g. Galatians and 2 Corinthians). This paradigm holds with the more personal letters as with the more corporate ones.

(In passing, it is worth noting that Hebrews, not thought to be written by Paul, lacks this salutation, but does end with 'Grace be with all of you.' And that there is no such sentence within 2 Corinthians, where some scholars think another letter from Paul has been incorporated, even though Paul makes many references to 'grace' in this letter.)

While it is true that other authors do send 'grace', it is not as noticeable or consistent, although, of course, we do not have such an extensive set for them (e.g. 1 Peter 1:2; 2 Peter 1:2; 2 John 1:3). The concluding 'grace' is also missing.

Romans 1:7 is typical: 'Grace to you and peace from God our Father and the Lord Jesus Christ.' It appears that Paul was combining a Jewish greeting (peace) with a standard Greek one. However, he changes the Greek *chaire*, which means 'rejoice' and has a different root, to *charis*, 'grace', although clearly there is a close verbal similarity. He may also have been adapting and incorporating the priestly blessing of Numbers 6:24–27, which refers to God's graciousness (not 'mercy') and peace. If so, he was emphasising the full incorporation of the Gentiles, since Numbers emphasises that this was for 'Israel'.

Another notable feature is that the words used at the beginning of each letter are more consistent than those with which he ends. No matter how challenging, or even strident, Paul's words might be, they are set within this context of grace.

4 Saved by grace

Ephesians 2:1–10

We turn now to the core of Paul's understanding of grace. Twice in these few verses Paul states most definitively that we are 'saved by grace': 'by grace you have been saved… by grace you have been saved through faith' (vv. 5, 8). For Paul it was not so much 'by faith alone' as 'by grace alone'.

Grace is not some vague abstract noun. It is the dynamic activity of God expressed by and through the life, death and resurrection of Jesus. Grace always has Jesus' face imprinted all over it. 'Jesus Christ is the incarnate Grace of God' (Barclay, p. 122).

Nor is it an automated process; it requires the total involvement and loving personal intervention of God in all his fullness. It is because God is 'rich in mercy' (v. 4) that we are saved by grace, not because God is simply just, let alone judgemental. It is out of the full reservoir of his personal love for us. And it demonstrates (perhaps for all the spiritual powers to see with unavoidable clarity!) 'the immeasurable riches of his grace' (v. 7). Again, we notice the exuberance of God's activity. It is riches, soaked in kindness. When Paul writes about God's saving grace, it is lyrical poetry, not cold logic, that sets the tone.

However, there is a spiritual logic involved. First, grace must be totally from God because of the incapacity of humans to do anything to restore the brokenness. We are 'dead through our trespasses' (v. 5). If God doesn't act, then no change is possible. Secondly, it must be God's doing, not ours, so that we cannot boast of it as our achievement. This is why Paul so vehemently insists that we are 'saved through faith', 'not the result of works' (vv. 8–9). Nowhere is this stated more clearly than Romans 11:6: 'If it is by grace, it is no longer on the basis of works, otherwise grace would no longer be grace.'

But it is much more than logic. For if human beings can save themselves, deal with their sin, restore the lost image, then Christ's death becomes unnecessary. This is the ultimate insult against God! Grace needs no supplements.

5 Serving grace

Ephesians 3:1–13

If this is the case, then the question thrusts itself on us, 'Shall we sin that grace may abound?' (see Romans 6:1, 15). Paul is emphatic that this is not possible, and if you think it is, you have not understood grace. For grace means we are called to live for God and are now free to do so: 'For we are... created in Christ Jesus for good works, which God prepared beforehand to be our way of life' (Ephesians 2:10).

The life we can now live is as much an outworking of God's grace as is our salvation! In Paul's case this was the commission God gave him to bring the good news to the Gentiles (v. 2). Paul explains why it is a matter of grace by referring to 'how the mystery was made known to me by revelation' (v. 3). Understandably such special revelation required divine initiative and so expressed God's grace.

Yet Paul's understanding seems broader than this. First, because he became 'a servant according to the gift of God's grace' (v. 7) that was given to him, but also because he received this commissioning even though 'I am the very least of all the saints' (v. 8). God's grace is seen in the state (or lack of status) of the person he chose, as well as in the way the commissioning was initiated.

Even more telling is Paul's claim in Ephesians 4 that 'each of us was given grace according to the measure of Christ's gift'; the ascended Christ 'gave gifts to his people' (vv. 7–8). This means that every Christian, including those who are Gentiles, has been given grace, or gracious gifts, through the generosity of the risen and ascended Christ. It is from this understanding that Paul moves on to explore and expound the multiplicity of 'gracious gifts' that the Spirit brings into the life of each Christian and the body of Christ (see, for instance, Romans 12:3–8; 1 Corinthians 12—14).

However, because these 'grace gifts' are just that (not rewards for trying hard, nor something we can claim is ours), they can never be used selfishly or for our aggrandisement. Nor can others' gifts be less valuable, because they are also gracious gifts from God!

6 Gifts of grace

Ephesians 4:1–13

Having emphasised the unity of the Christian community in verses 3–6, and used this as a motive for Christ-like behaviour in the previous verses, Paul then balances this with a recognition of the variety and differences within the church: 'But each of us was given grace [*charis*] according to the measure of Christ's gift' (v. 7). 1 Corinthians 12–14 indicates Paul was well aware that the gifts Christ gives (*charismata*) could become a source of envy, pride, contention and division.

The gifts he mentions here are the roles of 'apostles, prophets, evangelists, pastors and teachers' (v. 11). The emphasis is on the person fulfilling vital functions in the life of the church rather than on the gift itself (see Romans 12:6–8; 1 Corinthians 12–14; compare 1 Peter 4:10–11).

Of course, much has been written analysing the precise nature of these 'spiritual gifts', assessing how and when they should be used in the life of the church, and even whether they are valid expressions of the Holy Spirit's renewing activity or satanic counterfeits.

It is helpful to recall that just as the deeply Christocentric understanding of grace leads to practical, tangible expressions of grace, so here Paul is underlining that the variegated leadership of the church flows out of Christ's generosity. Christ's grace has practical, tangible outcomes. Grace may be theologically profound (see vv. 8–10), but it is essential to the proper sustaining and developing of the Christian community in its worship and mission. Both the use and appropriate exercise of these gifts, and their reception by the whole body, need to reflect their source in the generosity of the risen and ascended Saviour.

A few verses earlier, Paul reminded the Ephesians that their very salvation, which included their forgiveness, redemption and incorporation into the people of God, flowed out of the gift of God's grace: 'According to the gift of God's grace that was given to me… to bring to the Gentiles the news of the boundless riches of Christ' (3:7–8). Now he underlines that the purpose of these gifts of grace is to enable us all to know and become mature like Christ. Christ gave these gifts to equip and enable the church to do its job. They come from grace, they need to be used with grace, and they lead in to grace.

Guidelines

- Spend a few minutes meditating on the truths that a) Grace and truth come through Jesus Christ, and b) From his fullness we have all received grace upon grace.
- Recall times in your Christian journey when you have been especially conscious of this. Does a 'conversion experience' spring to mind? Or maybe a time when you know you let God down badly? Give thanks to God for his 'amazing grace' – perhaps listening to some songs about God's grace.
- Consider whether you would prefer to be judged by the law or grace. Do you think people outside the Christian faith appreciate that we are a 'grace-based faith'? If not, how might we show this (word, deeds, relationships) in our evangelism and mission?
- If you wanted to encourage people to understand that our faith is about God's grace in Jesus, which three stories from the gospels would you choose to tell them?
- We have seen that Paul's letters begin and end with grace, even though he can be extremely challenging and critical within these letters. How can we become a living example of grace, ensuring that every conversation, reaction and action is shot through with grace?
- Reread the parable of the prodigal son (Luke 15:11–32). Does this help us to distinguish mercy and grace? Does it matter that the word 'grace' isn't used? How does the father display grace to the older brother? What factors in the brother's life made it difficult for him to recognise and receive the superior way of grace?

1 Generous grace

2 Corinthians 8:1–11

At one level, 2 Corinthians 8—9 is about a very practical and down-to-earth issue: collecting money from the Asian churches and delivering it safely to the Jerusalem church to alleviate suffering, probably famine. They also show us Paul seeking to motivate the Corinthian Christians to become fully involved in this project and, behind this, his challenge to them to live out and fulfil their (boastful?) promises and their challenge to his authority. However, for Paul this process of giving is a deeply theological one, for he sees it as a clear expression of the heart of the gospel – grace. Because of the context, the NRSV frequently translates 'grace' as 'generous undertaking' or 'generous act'. This appropriately reflects the financial context but tends to dilute the theological depth.

This reaches its clearest expression in 8:9: 'For you know the generous act[a] of our Lord Jesus Christ, that though he was rich, yet for your sakes he became poor, so that by his poverty you might become rich.' The [a] indicates a footnote which says, 'the grace'. When Paul writes, 'you know', is he appealing to the Christian tradition which he had delivered to them, as in 1 Corinthians 11:23 (the Lord's supper) and 15:1–4 (the tradition concerning Christ's death and burial)? Either or both of these could be the substantive facts to which 'grace' refers, as could the whole process of incarnation as reflected in Philippians 2:6–8. He also appeals to their lived experience, understanding 'know' in the personal and intimate sense it can have.

The key understanding to which he appeals is the total sacrifice of Jesus ('though he was rich… he became poor'), together with the motivation ('for your sakes') and the outcome ('you might become rich'). Here, of course, Paul is not thinking of financial riches but spiritual riches: the spiritual riches of which the Corinthians might be tempted to boast (see 1 Corinthians 12—14), as well as their riches in being incorporated into the people of God.

This model of Jesus' grace at work will guide and modulate all that Paul has to say about Christian giving, as 9:11–13 makes clear.

2 Sustaining grace (the throne)

Hebrews 4:14–16

Hebrews is a book which emphasises the holiness of God as perceived in the Old Testament. The treatment of the tabernacles structure, the sacrificial system which required the shedding of blood and the role of the High Priest all emphasise this. But the emphatic, 'For indeed our God is a consuming fire' (12:29), together with the preceding verses, indicates that the author carried this sense of God's awesome otherness into their own understanding (see also 13:18–19). Acceptable worship requires reverence and awe.

Given this, it is all the more remarkable that God's throne is described as 'the throne of grace' (4:16). Even today, at the coronation of Charles III, his throne with its regal setting provided an imposing scene. This was far more intense in biblical times. Once on his throne, the despotic ruler demonstrated his superabundant wealth, his esteem among the nations and his unlimited power, and demanded total surrender – your life and death were in his hands.

The story of Esther provides us with helpful pictures of this reality. King Ahasuerus offers Esther half of his kingdom, yet this very generous offer is not really an act of grace, but prompted by her beauty: 'As soon as the king saw Queen Esther standing in the court, *she won his favour* and he held out to her the golden sceptre' (5:2 – my emphasis).

This is amplified in the visions in the book of Revelation, where God's throne is frequently referred to: 'At once I was in the spirit and there in heaven stood a throne, with one seated on the throne! And the one seated there looks like jasper and cornelian, and around the throne is a rainbow that looks like an emerald. Coming from the throne are flashes of lightning, and rumblings and peals… of thunder, and in front of the throne burn seven flaming torches, which are the seven spirits of God' (Revelation 4:2–5). This awe-inspiring vision is the 'throne of grace'.

In contrast, God's throne is truly a throne of grace because his unbounded generosity is his response to our need and sinfulness, not because of our dedicated obedience or Christ-like character.

3 Sustaining grace (the grounds)

Hebrews 4:14–16

We are encouraged to approach this throne, not with fear and apprehension but with 'boldness' (v. 16). How on earth can we realistically approach the divine throne with boldness, sinful, mortal and weak as we are? 'Boldness' could suggest that we do this because of some inherent quality in us. This is not at all the position of this letter, and many translations prefer 'with confidence'.

As a police chaplain, I have a pass which gives me entrance to every police station in the county. It's not because of my inherent worth, but because I have been granted permission, that I can approach any station with confidence.

The word also implies openness. I don't need to approach from the side, hoping I won't be spotted; indeed, if this is my attitude, it suggests I have misunderstood the invitation. Nor do I need to express my request obliquely – I can be straight to the point.

The grounds for this appeal are all to do with the reality of Jesus: who he is, what he has experienced during his earthly life, and now his position in the heavens. Primarily, it is because Jesus knows all the challenges of being human that we can be sure he understands our present needs and is able to sympathise. He has been 'tested as we are' (v. 15).

This is an observation which has already been established. Jesus' total identity with our humanity means that he experienced the full range of human emotions, including fear and suffering. This suffering culminated in his death; through this he tasted death for everyone (2:9) and so freed us all from the fear of death, which holds us in slavery, ultimately to the devil (2:13; see also the oblique reference to Jesus' struggle in Gethsemane, 5:7–9).

It is Jesus' position in the heavens, his public acceptance and acclamation by the Father, which ground the confidence we can have (see 10:19–23), and 'he is able for all time/completely to save those who approach God through him, since he always lives to make intercession for them' (7:25).

4 Sufficient grace

2 Corinthians 12:1–10

A serious physical problem, a source of Satan's devious cruelty – but also something God was using! When Paul introduces this thorn, he states, 'a thorn was given to me in the flesh' (v. 7). This is 'a divine passive' – a way of acknowledging that God was ultimately involved in the process.

All three dimensions above need to be taken into account if we are to appreciate how God's grace can be sufficient in situations where there is apparently no positive answer. When, for instance, much prayer is offered, much faith exercised and no healing comes. When a family sits through endless days and nights watching their father die, having been summoned three weeks before because his death was imminent. When that question, 'Why?', beats in our hearts like a tiresome drum.

What does it mean to hear God say, 'My grace is sufficient for you'?

First, Paul is reminded that God is bigger than even this significant and debilitating problem. In many situations Paul had faced apparently insurmountable problems that appeared to shatter both his life and his ministry. A notable example was his imprisonment with Silas in the Philippian jail. But then, in a huge variety of ways, God had broken through. It is one thing to experience this, and life experience can help us through overwhelming difficulties. But it is another to hear God speak into our lives, 'My grace is sufficient for you.'

Second, we can remind ourselves that God is able to use our trying and apparently destructive experiences for our good and the good of others around us. Paul was able to discern, in part at least, God's purpose. It was to keep him from being 'too elated' (v. 7). This suffering was not ultimately pointless. Praying for understanding as to how on earth this suffering can have any good in it is part of discovering the sufficiency of God's grace.

Third, we can experience more of Christ, 'so that the power of Christ may dwell in me' (v. 9). Paul gave everything to serve the gospel, but in this situation he embraced the reality that in the end it was up to God alone to sustain him and bring fruitfulness.

Finally, rather than intensifying our suffering by self-doubt and questioning, we can use even this as an opportunity to bear testimony to his sufficient grace – 'I will boast all the more gladly of my weaknesses' (v. 9).

5 Future grace

1 Peter 1:4–21

This passage introduces us to the future dimension of grace: 'Set all your hope on the grace that Jesus Christ will bring you when he is revealed' (1 Peter 1:13). Clearly this implies that the grace of Jesus is neither only a present lived experience for the believer nor limited to Christ's saving action whilst living out his human life, death and resurrection.

This future eschatological dimension of grace is depicted in verses 4 and 5: 'An inheritance that is imperishable, undefiled, and unfading, kept in heaven for you, who are being protected by the power of God through faith for a salvation ready to be revealed in the last time.'

The concept of inheritance is biblically rich. It runs through the Old Testament, where the land is the inheritance passed on via the promise given to Abraham, for instance, but could also be God himself (Psalm 16:5). It is also a powerful image in the New Testament. The privilege involved is summarised well in Ephesians 1:19 and worked through by Paul in Romans 8. Though inheritance necessarily involves death for the inheritor to receive anything, this passage also emphasises the grace-like quality of it all, as the inheritance is given, not earned.

Peter uses three words to underline the security of this inheritance: imperishable, undefiled and unfading. These three resounding words emphasise that although future, this grace is not subject to catastrophes, human sin or even the transitoriness of all earthly life. To underline this, it is 'kept in heaven' (v. 4). Their availability and accessibility do not depend on our ability.

So what is the believers' contribution? What does it mean to set all our hope on this amazing grace, and to do so unreservedly? The rest of the letter expounds this. This hope is to be the focus and primary motivation: to be holy, to get rid of all malice, to abstain from the desires of the flesh. This future aspect of grace is the stimulus and grounds to live fully dedicated Christian lives. Grace not only saves us and supports us when life is challenging, nor is it only a model for our way to live. It is also the driver to be fully Christ-like.

6 The supreme grace

2 Corinthians 13:1–13

Verse 13 here is the basis for the 'grace' often shared in church: 'The grace of the Lord Jesus Christ, the love of God, and the communion of the Holy Spirit be with all of you.' Although well-known and frequently said by congregations to each other, it would be foolish to allow familiarity to breed contempt. For these words are theologically profound and pastorally challenging, with significant mission implications.

Paul has challenged the Christians in Corinth about serious moral issues, appealed for unity, defended his authority, explained the gospel and spiritual gifts, and challenged them about giving. The church community seemed difficult in many ways. When he says, 'be with *all* of you' (emphasis mine), this in itself is a profound example of grace.

But the theological issues associated with this verse are also significant. We consider only two. First, the order of Son, God, Holy Spirit is surprising to some. Many commentators would agree that Paul had not developed a fully worked-out doctrine of the Trinity, as was to become a fascination within the later early church, but would also recognise that the basic ingredients for such developments are in embryonic form here. Perhaps the very order reflects Paul as a passionate apostle of the gospel and not a theoretical theologian.

C.K. Barrett summarises a rationale for this order well: 'Behind the *grace of the Lord Jesus Christ*, which is known as an observable event in history, stands *the love of God*, which though commended in the action and especially the death of Jesus (Rom. v. 8) is an eternal fact' (p. 344).

Second, we need to consider whether these genitives are subjective or objective. Most commentators accept that 'the grace of the Lord Jesus Christ' means the grace which Jesus has or does show towards others. Equally, most accept that 'the love of God' means the love God has for us, which he has shown through his saving activity in Jesus, and not our love for God. When we come to the 'the communion of the Holy Spirit' there is less agreement, as the footnote in the NRSVA indicates – 'Or *and the sharing in*'. Does Paul mean 'the fellowship which the Holy Spirit creates and sustains' or 'the sharing in the life of the Holy Spirit' which the Corinthians claim is so vital? Perhaps both are equally valid and necessary.

Guidelines

- What difference does it make to the way we exercise our ministry to constantly recall that it is a '*gift* of God's grace'? For instance, that our ministry is not our right or duty but a privilege? Do we take enough time to thank God for his calling and to surrender it to him?
- How can we ensure that we exercise this gift appropriately? Do we recognise that it is not a reward for holiness or even natural competences or learning?
- Do we recognise that God's grace has been given to us to spread the 'boundless riches of Christ'? What would you include in the 'boundless riches'?
- How can we help our congregations share in this mission task with us? How much of what we do as church makes these riches available?
- Reflect on times when you have prayed earnestly and persistently for things in your life to be dealt with so that you could be released from their draining impact on you. Were these primarily physical, spiritual, moral or emotional?
    - Did you gain encouragement to continue in your praying from verses like Luke 11:5–10, John 14:13–14 and Ephesians 6:18?
    - What, in the end, led to you ceasing to pray for this release? Did you lose heart? Find it less painful to stop than continuing to hope? Get a sense from God that he was saying 'trust me to deal with it'?
- Have you experienced God calling you to pray for someone with a chronic condition over a long period of time? Or is there someone you could do this for?

FURTHER READING

W. Barclay, *The Mind of St Paul* (Collins, 1958).

C. K. Barrett, *The Second Epistle to the Corinthians (Blacks NT Commentaries)* (London, 1982).

Max Lucado, *In the Grip of Grace* (Word Publishing, 1996).

John Oman, *Grace and Personality (The Fontana Library)* (Collins, 1962).

C. R. Smith, *The Biblical Doctrine of Grace* (The Epworth Press, 1956).

2 Samuel 11—24: David the king: failure and fallout

Walter Moberly

In the previous issue we read 2 Samuel 1—10, with its account of David's victory in a civil war with the house of Saul. David captured Jerusalem to be the capital for his kingdom. He achieved military ascendancy over the Philistines and other warring neighbours. With one or two exceptions, not least his failure to discipline his unruly commander Joab for the murder of Abner, it is a story that paints David in a positive light as a man led by God. There is a high point in God's promise to him of an enduring dynasty (2 Samuel 7). Chapter 10 ends with David standing tall. But the note on which our reading ended was the Pauline warning: 'If you think you are standing, watch out that you do not fall' (1 Corinthians 10:12).

The continuing story is remarkable. Most nations like to present their heroes in a favourable light, with weaknesses and failures perhaps noted but pushed to the margins. David, Israel's greatest king, has his faithless and ruthless actions put centre-stage by the biblical writer. His sin is depicted unsparingly, and it paves the way for the sequence of family tragedies that will follow in its train. A subplot revolves around David's cousin and commander, Joab, who is reminiscent of the kind of character we see in a movie like *The Godfather*. Again, the biblical writer resists any sugar-coating of harsh realities.

Open-eyed recognition of the devastation that can be brought about by self-serving priorities and the misuse of power is what the biblical writer gives us. And it centres on the man who is said to be 'a man after God's own heart' (1 Samuel 13:14). Prayerful pondering of this material is a painful, but important, spiritual discipline. Yet in and through it all we see people for whom God cares, and through whom God's good purposes continue to be at work.

Bible quotations are taken from the NRSV.

1 When sin snowballs

2 Samuel 11

It all begins with a simple, probably unthinking, failure of duty. One of the prime duties of an ancient king was to lead his people in warfare (v. 1). Yet for some unspecified reason, David sends Joab in his place. He was also having an unduly long siesta if it went on till late afternoon (v. 2; the Hebrew word is in fact 'evening'). David was not lacking available women (3:2–5; 5:13), so why did the sight of a beautiful woman bathing make him feel frisky? Overall, David appears to have felt deeply out of sorts. But instead of handling it sensibly and responsibly (and we remember how his ability at music-making helped a troubled Saul, 1 Samuel 16:14–23; why not for himself too?), he shuts out God and his conscience. Never mind if Bathsheba is the wife of one of his soldiers: he has the power to take her, and she has a certain novelty value to perhaps help relieve his mood.

But then it spirals. Bathsheba becomes pregnant, and David wants to try to conceal his adulterous responsibility for this. However, Uriah acts with consistent integrity. He will not feast or enjoy his wife while his fellow soldiers are in the field of battle. And when the king's insistence means that he must feast, he at least remains abstinent with what is still in his control (vv. 6–13).

For David, Uriah does not command respect or bring any self-reproach. Rather, Uriah has made himself into a problem that needs drastic resolution. This brings in the loyal, but amoral, Joab, who is happy to help his master, no questions asked. A simple strategy then brings about Uriah's death. But it is not just Uriah who dies, as a number of other soldiers are also killed – needlessly, as an approach to the walls of a besieged city was always risky, as Joab observes, and maybe unnecessary (many sieges were a matter of sitting it out, inside and outside the city, and the side which ran out of food first lost). But murderous folly can easily be rationalised by David as the fortunes of war (vv. 14–25). And his lust for Bathsheba can be regularised (vv. 26–27).

Tragedy begins when David, previously open to God, closes his heart both to God and to those around him.

2 The wages of sin

2 Samuel 12:1–25

How do you communicate with those who don't want to hear? I find myself asking this question when I periodically hear a certain street-preacher in Durham, who faithfully uses the language of the New Testament and Protestant theology, yet seems to make no impact whatever on passers-by. There are no easy answers. Yet a more imaginative approach (as, say, in some street-theatre) can sometimes get through to the otherwise heedless. Certainly the prophet Nathan exemplifies the power of imaginatively reworking an issue. David's conscience had been sleepily inoperative, but had not disappeared, and is aroused by Nathan in such a way as to open himself to the unforgettable, 'You are the man!' (vv. 1–7a).

Nathan's continuing message from the Lord focuses initially on David's sheer ingratitude for all that the Lord had done for him (vv. 7b–8). David's cruel resort to deceptive and murderous violence, heedless of God's ways and priorities, will now mean that what David inflicted on Uriah will now be inflicted on him; as he has sown, so will he reap (vv. 9–10). Further, the sexual use of a woman that David had thought could be kept private will now take on a harshly public dimension in future. Not only David but also others will now suffer from what he has unleashed (vv. 11–12). The consequences of David's sin will unfold in the chapters that follow.

David now sees what he has done and acknowledges it (vv. 13a). Indeed, the Hebrew text indicates a pause, in the form of a paragraph marker, mid-verse, immediately after David's words. This may well imply: Think/recite Psalm 51 at this point.

David receives mercy: he will not die. Yet the fate of the child still links the wages of sin with death. The child clearly matters to David, given the urgency of his self-denial and intercession. Yet it is all in vain. David then surprises his servants with his apparent lack of mourning. But what mattered had been present in his pleading. David accepts its failure and seeks to move on (vv. 13b–23).

An astonishing sign of grace then comes in the Lord's favour shown to the next child of David and Bathsheba (vv. 24–25). In a sense, Solomon should never have been born. Yet God specially cares for him, and will give him a major role for his life. God's ways are greater than human messiness and failure.

3 Tragedies begin to unfold

2 Samuel 13

It is striking how the biblical writers are happy to use weighty words that depict great realities with the same breadth of meaning as in common parlance, which can use them trivially. Amnon 'loved' (v. 1), while Jonadab was 'wise' (v. 3). The NRSV tries to indicate the sense in context with 'fell in love with' and 'was crafty', which is fine; though arguably the sense is really 'was lustfully infatuated with' and 'was deviously cunning'. The realities of love and wisdom are here shown in utterly corrupt form.

The narrative flows relentlessly from lust to lies to rape to the contemptuous dismissal of the despairing Tamar (vv. 4–19). Amnon's change of attitude can perhaps seem surprising, but the psychological dynamic is perfectly captured by Shakespeare in his Sonnet 129:

The expense of spirit in a waste of shame / Is lust in action...
Enjoy'd no sooner but despiséd straight; / Past reason hunted; and no sooner had,
Past reason hated, as a swallow'd bait, / On purpose laid to make the taker mad.

Tamar is left desolate. David, although angry, does precisely nothing. Apart from his own previous actions leaving him with little moral authority, some ancient manuscripts add a clarification that David was a poor father willing to indulge a favourite child (v. 21). Sadly, David learns nothing here as he subsequently behaves similarly with Adonijah (1 Kings 1:6).

Absalom nurses his resentment. He waits a couple of years, so that his proposed invitation to a formal seasonal celebration would not seem suspicious. One may wonder whether Absalom was counting on his father declining the invitation, as that might make it harder for David to object to Amnon, as eldest son and heir to the throne, going instead. David too readily lets any sensible reservation be overcome by Absalom's persistence (vv. 23–27). The result is unsurprising. The virtue of 'courage' is now shown in corrupt form, as a drunken Amnon is murdered by Absalom's retainers (vv. 28–29).

The news travels fast in garbled form. Although Jonadab eases the king's worst fears, his accurate perception indicates that he was a faithless friend to Amnon in not ensuring that he kept away from Absalom. Again, David does nothing except weep, apparently as much for the murderous Absalom as the murdered Amnon (vv. 30–39). Responsible disciplinary action has become too much for the king who has lost his way and is thereby losing his family.

4 Re-enter Absalom, exit David

2 Samuel 14:25—15:23

We pass over Joab's stratagem to get Absalom back from Geshur, his mother's original home, to which he had fled (3:3; 13:37; 14:23), though David retains some authority by keeping Absalom at a distance (14:1–24).

We learn three things initially about Absalom. First, not only is he good-looking, but he is also narcissistic about it as he takes the trouble to weigh his cut hair (14:25–27). Secondly, when Joab fails to get Absalom fully restored to his father's presence, Absalom ruthlessly plays hardball with his benefactor until he gets what he wants (14:28–33). Thirdly, he claims executive royalty, whether by having a huge escort of macho men, or by promising justice to those in need (which implies that David had become lax and negligent here), or by general schmoozing (15:1–6).

Absalom is then entirely happy to use the language of religious devotion deceitfully, to lull any suspicions his father might have had (15:7–9). In Hebron he has sufficient freedom of action to launch his bid for full kingly power. People rally to him, and he secures the services of Ahithophel, perhaps a kind of ancient Henry Kissinger (15:10–12; also 16:23).

It is not clear that David's decision to flee Jerusalem was a good one, as it should usually be easier to defend a city from within than have to survive and fight somewhere in the open. But maybe David feared that he could no longer count on the loyalty of those within the city. Anyway, no one tries to argue with him, and his officials still take his orders (15:13–18). ('Where was Joab?' one might wonder. Although we will see later that he accompanied David, silence about him here might perhaps suggest that Joab was unsure which horse to back.)

The narrative that unfolds in the following chapters is hardly about military strategy or tactics. Rather, it is about encounters between people, mostly David and a wide range of others. The handling of interpersonal relationship and responsibility in the extreme pressure and conflict of civil war is the focus of interest.

First is Ittai. As 'Gittite' means 'from Gath', Ittai was a Philistine. David clearly had the ability to attract people across conventional boundaries. Despite David's considering him a free agent, Ittai is bound by deep loyalty to his Israelite king. He displays costly faithfulness (15:19–23).

5 David as faithful yet foolish

2 Samuel 15:24—16:14

As David flees Jerusalem, he refuses to use the ark superstitiously as a kind of safety charm (as Israel once had, 1 Samuel 4:1–11). His basic spiritual intuition remains healthy, and so he entrusts himself directly to his Lord. Yet sending the priests back to Jerusalem can also serve a further useful purpose: David might gain insider information from Jerusalem through their sons. It is a sensible strategy (15:24–29).

David goes up the Mount of Olives, between Jerusalem and the wilderness, weeping and praying. When he hears of the disloyalty of the valued Ahithophel, he prays a specific prayer, that Ahithophel's wisdom will become destructive foolishness that will bring down both him and Absalom. And when he prays, indeed at a special place of worship (unexplained) at the top of the Mount, the answer to his prayer immediately meets him: his friend Hushai, in whose loyalty he still trusts. David asks Hushai to play the high-risk role of pretending to defect to Absalom, so that he can counter Ahithophel. David already intuits that an answer to his prayer need not in fact be that Ahithophel should become foolish, but rather that any wise advice he gives should be countered and disregarded (15:30–37). Prayer can be answered in more than one way.

Ziba's provisions would no doubt have been welcome to David. But David allows his own wisdom to become folly in believing Ziba's far-fetched claim about Mephibosheth's hope that Absalom was doing all this not for himself but so as to restore the house of Saul to the throne. David, in his grief and upset, might not be in a good frame of mind. But to fail to smell any possible rat in Ziba's account of his disabled master, or take advice from anyone around him before rewarding Ziba at Mephibosheth's expense, indicates a foolish impetuousness (16:1–4). Ziba's loyalty to David may opportunistically conceal a deeper disloyalty to his abandoned master.

As if David was not already in sufficient distress, the forbidding figure of Shimei, wildly assaulting David with both words and stones, could serve to make his misery complete (16:5–8). Though Abishai, Joab's brother, suggests a cutting-edge resolution in characteristic family mode, David resolves to bear it all as part of his affliction. His tone sounds a bit fatalistic, yet despite everything he retains a trusting hope that the Lord may yet bring good out of the mess.

6 The clash between Hushai and Ahithophel

2 Samuel 16:15—17:23

The camera lens, as it were, of the narrator leaves the weary David at the Jordan and zooms back to Jerusalem. It is here that the outcome of the civil war will be resolved.

Two preliminaries set the scene. First, Hushai has to commend himself to Absalom, who is not unreasonably suspicious of Hushai's shift of allegiance. Hushai's poker-faced lying is strengthened by appealing to the Lord's will. In a narrative where the Lord's action is overall low-key, devout-sounding appeals to the Lord will appear regularly (e.g. Absalom, 15:7–8; Shimei, 16:8). It is painful, but realistic, to recognise that sometimes the language of faith is used to make a lie more persuasive – and Hushai does not blink (16:15–19).

Second, the first thing that Ahithophel advises is, surprisingly, nothing to do with pursuing David. Rather he commends an action that is clearly heavily symbolic, perhaps as marking a point of no return. At our cultural distance today, it is hard to catch the precise significance of Absalom's having sex (presumably rather hurriedly) with his father's concubines, whose status in relation to David's wives is also elusive. Yet, as similarly on the part of Abner (3:6–7), there seems to be an implication of claiming royal power (perhaps because only kings enjoyed a harem), quite apart from Nathan's forewarning it (12:11). Certainly, if Ahithophel commends it, nobody questions it (16:20–23).

The key issue is what Absalom's next step will be. Ahithophel advises swift and immediate pursuit, with the killing of David as the straightforward way to victory. Hushai speaks at greater length to make the opposite case: Don't tangle with an enraged David, but rather take time to gather a large army and thereby ensure victory (17:1–13). We are then told what we might have inferred anyway from the preceding narrative, that Ahithophel's was the better course of action. There is also the all-important note that the setting-aside of Ahithophel's counsel was the Lord's doing (17:14; in answer to David's prayer, 15:31).

Hushai then warns David to move on (presumably lest Absalom change his mind), using David's strategy for getting information about what was going on in Jerusalem (17:15–22). Ahithophel now reckons Absalom's cause is likely to fail, and/or has a fit of resentful sulks at this presumably unprecedented ignoring of his advice. Either way, his departure and suicide look like a nail in Absalom's coffin also (17:23).

Guidelines

The note about the Lord's special love for Solomon (12:24–25) merits some further reflection.

In terms of the remainder of 2 Samuel, it is perhaps surprising since Solomon does not feature at all. He next appears in 1 Kings 1, in the account of the struggle over who will succeed the dying David. Many interpreters have inferred from this that the note about the Lord's love for Solomon plays a structuring role in the overall story that follows. Sons of David who were older than Solomon, and so more likely to succeed their father, are all displaced – first Amnon, then Absalom, finally Adonijah. Thus Solomon succeeds David. This is surely a fruitful reading as an example of how God's providence can work out.

Beyond the immediate narrative there are also wider implications, as noted briefly on Day 2. Solomon's birth was not the fruit of healthy marital love, the burgeoning of that love into new life. Although David had married Bathsheba prior to Solomon's birth and may have loved her (though we are not told so), their marriage and its fruit are bound up with lust, adultery and murder. Yet the Lord loves their child and gives him a special name, Jedidiah ('Beloved of the Lord'), that expresses this, though interestingly this name, while recorded, is never used in the story.

In a contemporary context, many births are not the fruit of healthy love. For many and complex reasons, some children are born into unstable situations, and sometimes as they grow up they realise that their birth was the result not of stable fruit-seeking love but of casual lust, and that their birth was, humanly, an unwanted accident. Such awareness can be hard to live with and can seem to call in question the value of their life.

Our biblical passage reminds us that, with God, no life is an unwanted accident, as his providence, his good purposes, go deeper than human weakness and failure. Of course, if talk of providence is not to be mere words, faithful people who trust that providence need to embody it and live it out. Thereby it can become reality for those who might otherwise struggle to accept that goodness and purpose are indeed the bottom line for understanding themselves and living well in God's world.

1 The death of Absalom

2 Samuel 17:24—18:18

Once in Transjordan, and at some space from Absalom and his troops, David finds a friendly reception at Mahanaim. We also learn the interesting detail that Absalom's chief of staff is Amasa, who is also part of David's wider family, a cousin both to Absalom and to Joab and Abishai (the text of verse 25 is difficult, but 1 Chronicles 2:13–17 clarifies). He will be significant later in the story. This civil war is really a family war (17:24–29).

Three things stand out in the preparations for battle. First, the loyal Philistine Ittai is rewarded by sharing command with Joab and Abishai. Second, David himself will not go, at his troops' request. Their valuing of David is legitimate; but David's acceding to their request is a sign that he is no longer the warrior he once was. Third, David gives instructions about being merciful to Absalom that become known to all his troops (18:1–5). The main battle that follows is of little interest to the narrator, apart from an intriguing note about the dangerous terrain (18:6–8).

The focus is on Absalom. It is unclear whether his being trapped in a tree is because of his extensive hair (14:26; with a possible implication of pride leading to humiliation) or, probably more likely, that his head got caught in entangling branches. Either way, he is left helpless. The ensuing dialogue between the soldier and Joab sharply captures the existential dynamic of the moment. The soldier is fearful because of David's instructions, and not unreasonably reckons that if he had killed Absalom he would have been abandoned to a deadly fate himself. Joab, however, thinks only in hard-nosed military terms: the death of Absalom will bring victory and an end to the revolt, as indeed it does. So he takes the lead in killing Absalom, though the contributory action of his companions perhaps ensures that no one person can be held responsible for the killing (18:9–17).

This section ends with the sad note about Absalom's seeking remembrance by setting up a pillar. Earlier, we have been told about Absalom having three sons (14:27); but they had probably, like so many, died in infancy, leaving him bereft. Unlike his father David, who is remembered for his faith in God, Absalom is remembered as a vain and impatient man who set his heart on power and lost everything.

2 When is good news bad news?

2 Samuel 18:19—19:8a

Joab understands the implications of what he has done in a way that others appear not to. Ahimaaz, who earlier had brought warning to David (17:15–21), supposes that news of victory will be welcome to the king, and probably also that the bearer of such good news will be rewarded. Joab warns him against this, and sends a non-Israelite, a Cushite, instead. Joab reckons that the bearer of the bad news of Absalom's death may likely suffer for it; and he considers a Cushite to be more expendable than an Israelite. Ahimaaz, however, persists, perhaps reckoning that if he can offer a selective account of the victory he will indeed receive a reward. So Joab shrugs and lets him get on with it (18:19–23).

David watches and waits, and receives news of runners. News of the outcome of a battle was typically carried by a runner (presumably horses were often scarce; Absalom had ridden a mule in battle). Best known is the story of Pheidippides running to Athens with the news of the Athenian victory over the Persians at Marathon in 490BC, a distance memorialised in marathons today. David has high hopes of Ahimaaz, who indeed brings only good news of victory by falsely concealing the fact that Absalom is dead. The Cushite is initially as circumspect as Ahimaaz, mentioning only victory, but is then more honest in saying what Ahimaaz would not, and apparently does not suffer for it (18:24–32).

For David, victory is swallowed up by death. He thinks only of 'my son' as personal tragedy consumes him. His overwhelming grief affects his soldiers too (18:33—19:4). Joab, however, is unimpressed. In political and military terms, he had done what needed to be done to remove a usurper and restore David to his throne. So he lashes out at David, calling him blindly ungrateful for all that his soldiers have done for him. Indeed, he issues an ultimatum to David, that unless David goes out and greets and thanks his troops he, Joab, will abandon David, taking the army with him, and leave him worse off than when Absalom first rebelled (19:5–7).

The threat works. David goes out to the troops and a semblance of normality is restored (19:8). David probably realises that if Absalom is dead, it is Joab's doing: Joab has form. But he says nothing and simply complies with his commander, who now calls the shots.

3 The slow road back to Jerusalem

2 Samuel 19:8b—30

There is an initial note about nervousness among many Israelites. They reasonably reckon that they are in trouble for having supported Absalom, and want to regain David's favour by helping his return to Jerusalem and his throne. David responds to this by prodding his own southern tribe of Judah – among whom Absalom had begun his revolt in Hebron – into some constructive competition with the northerners. As both north and south have some egg on their faces after David's victory, let each outdo the other in renewing their services to their king (vv. 8b–12)!

David also, at last, decides to do something about Joab. For now, Joab has humiliated David by ignoring his clear order and killing his cherished son, and by ordering David around. So David turns to another family member, Amasa, to replace Joab as army commander. This also, of course, makes political sense as a gesture to the Israelites who had supported Absalom, if their commander (17:25) is now to be David's commander. This looks like a constructive move of reconciliation, and Amasa acts swiftly and well (vv. 13–15).

Shimei and Ziba, who have guilty consciences, move with speed to greet the victorious David, bringing some back-up with them (vv. 16–18a). Shimei realises that his cursing and stone-throwing mean that his prospects aren't great, and he grovels. Abishai responds with characteristic advice, which one might well expect David to go with. David, however, recognises that if he has received grace beyond expectation, he should rightly extend this to others too. So Shimei is spared (vv. 18b–23).

David knows Ziba's story, so he speaks to Mephibosheth, who has also come to meet him. David wants to know why only Ziba, and not Mephibosheth also, joined him when he was fleeing. Mephibosheth explains that Ziba tricked him, leaving him without transport. The clue that Mephibosheth is telling the truth is twofold. First, he has lived as if in deep mourning since David left Jerusalem (v. 24). Secondly, he responds to David's dividing of his goods with a gesture similar to that of the true mother of the living child before Solomon (v. 30; compare 1 Kings 3:26).

David, however, fails to recognise honest loyalty when he sees it, and weakly allows Ziba to get away with his treachery. The responsibility to discern justly is absent in a diminished David.

4 The wisdom of Barzillai the Gileadite

2 Samuel 19:31–43

Barzillai, though wealthy, was an ordinary man who lived a quiet life well away from the centre of events in Jerusalem. His moment of fame, as part of the story of King David, is, in human terms, accidental. He happened to be in the right place at the right time, without having planned it. He and others had generously provided for David when he was first in Transjordan, at Mahanaim (17:27–29). Now he has been one of those escorting David to the river Jordan. So David wants to show his gratitude by making Barzillai an honoured guest back at his court in Jerusalem.

Barzillai declines graciously. His basic reason is simple. At his age, his faculties are declining. Fine food and drink are wasted on him, and his hearing has become so poor that fine singing is also wasted on him. He also feels unworthy of such reward when he had only done what came naturally to him. So he wants to live out his remaining days in his own home, near those family graves that symbolise part of his identity. It is a winsome picture of contentment in ageing decline, more hopeful than Shakespeare's harsher, 'Last scene of all, / That ends this strange eventful history, / Is second childishness and mere oblivion…' (from Jaques' 'Seven Ages of Man' in *As You Like It*). The last stages of life can indeed be harsh, but Barzillai reminds that they are not necessarily so, and can be moments of grace in their own way. When so much contemporary life seeks novelty and fears death, this is a picture to ponder.

Nonetheless, Barzillai sees that David's gratitude opens an opportunity for someone else: Chimham (pronounced 'kimham'). Some ancient manuscripts add the clarification that Chimham is Barzillai's son, though this is not included in the NRSV. David is happy with such an arrangement, and there is evidence that it was enduring. In Jeremiah 41:17 there is mention of a place, Geruth Chimham ('Chimham's holding') near Bethlehem, which likely indicates a land grant that David made to Chimham. David, though diminished, still makes his gratitude count. Barzillai, though firm in his Gileadite roots, enables his son to settle and live elsewhere.

The chapter ends with a reminder of continuing squabbles between northerners (Israelites) and southerners (Judahites), jockeying for position over what they had done for David. The Barzillai episode reminds us of a better way.

5 Joab strikes again

2 Samuel 20:1–25

The squabbles between northerners and southerners, just mentioned (19:41–43), now break out into something more serious. Sheba, a Benjaminite (and so from King Saul's tribe), starts another rebellion, which could become yet another civil war (vv. 1–2). Allegiance to David might be more fragile than suggested.

In an initial note, however, David, like Absalom, attends first to his concubines (if only we could discern the full significance of this prioritising!). He ensures that they are safe and provided for (v. 3). Yet it is hard not to feel that their subsequent enclosure is a human tragedy (akin to that of Tamar, 13:20) which exemplifies the knock-on impact on others of David's earlier faithlessness.

David tells his new commander, Amasa, to get troops from Judah (which should be mainly loyal to him) to counter Sheba's threat. We are not told why Amasa falls behind schedule, but the result is that David, clearly wanting speedy action, turns to the experienced Abishai. Hindsight is, of course, 20/20, but it is hard not to question David's wisdom here. It is unsurprising that Joab accompanies his brother. And when they encounter Amasa, Joab treats this rival to his power in the same way he had treated Abner (3:27). Since the sight of Amasa's corpse brings soldiers to a halt, as had Asahel's earlier (2:23) – presumably from a respect for the dead – one of Joab's men just bundles him out of the way and out of sight, with no respect whatever, so that they can get on with things. Joab is back in charge (vv. 4–13).

The conflict with Sheba turns into a siege. But although the practicalities of siege warfare are duly noted (v. 15), all interest focuses on a conversation between Joab and a 'wise' woman, which in this context seems to mean someone with a local reputation as the go-to person for advice. She also appeals to her town's reputation for providing good advice, with the implication that Joab should not destroy such a valuable Israelite town (vv. 18–19). A simple expedient is decided on: the people in the town execute Sheba and give Joab his head (to take back to David in Jerusalem as evidence of success?). The short-lived rebellion comes to an end (vv. 14–22).

The final list of David's officials is contextually weighty (vv. 23–26). Lead position is held by Joab, now again army commander, and beyond David's control.

6 David's last words

2 Samuel 23:1–7

There is interesting, and sometimes difficult, material about David in chapters 21—24 which we must pass over. It will be appropriate to finish our reading of David's story with what are explicitly ascribed to him as 'last words'. How these relate to the narrative of David and his deathbed words in 1 Kings 1:1—2:11 is unclear. Presumably they are like our notion of a last will and testament, i.e. a final formal statement rather than actual last words uttered.

The overall sense of the psalm-like poem is clear, though some of the Hebrew is difficult, and translations have some striking variations. This is particularly so in verse 1, where NRSV's 'the favourite of the Strong One of Israel' replaces 'the sweet psalmist of Israel' of older translations (AV, RSV). 'Sweet singer' is still a perfectly acceptable rendering of the Hebrew. It reminds us of what has been an absence throughout the David narrative of 2 Samuel, with the possible exception of David's lament over Saul and Jonathan, and the summarising psalm of the preceding chapter, 2 Samuel 22. No psalm is seen or heard. The narrative account of David is thus one-sided in terms of his enduring significance. For the deep connection between David and the psalms has been at the heart of much understanding and use of the Old Testament down the centuries. The psalms play a key role in thinking about David not just as a king, but as a fallible man of God.

After the introduction (v. 1) there are three emphases. First, the divine spirit speaking through David specifies the key quality of the true king/leader: that he exercises power justly, knowing himself to be accountable to God (vv. 2–3). Such integrity in practice is always like the beginning of a beautiful day (v. 4), for it goes a long way towards enabling life to be what it should be.

Second, David celebrates God's enduring covenantal commitment to him and his house, as announced by the prophet Nathan in 2 Samuel 7 (v. 5). This is a commitment where grace is greater than all human weakness and failure.

Third, David speaks of the bleak prospects of the godless (vv. 6–7).

We have seen numerous practical qualifications to these. Nonetheless, they remain a moral and spiritual vision that is a fine swan song for David, the man exalted by God.

Guidelines

One of the questions to ponder as we come to the end of our reading is: What kind of man was David?

There is a natural tendency in Christian faith to talk in terms of polarities: good and evil, right and wrong, believer and unbeliever, saint and sinner. Although such language has its place, a study of David underlines what we discover in life: many people are decidedly mixed. There are strong positives in David: a man after God's own heart, courageous victor over Goliath, a heroic fugitive, the sweet singer, the chosen recipient of God's promise. Yet we also see someone who kills many, takes numerous wives (none of whom he is said to love), is an adulterer and murderer, is a poor father, and who increasingly loses control both of his family and of his kingdom.

A classic principle, evident in the canonisation of saints, is that you must wait until after death, until a life can be seen as a whole, before making whatever overall judgement may appropriately be made about that life; although only God sees with full clarity. David's life, a good part of which we have been reading, can be seen as a whole. Would David qualify for canonisation? I imagine not. There are too many strikes against him. Yet the Old Testament gives more space to King David than to anyone else (Moses included), and so he is presumably of high importance for understanding Israel and its faith.

David shows us something of the mysterious depths of what it is to be human, and specifically to be a sinful human who yet knows himself bound to God as his Lord and master. His commitment to God does not whitewash all that is questionable in his life and his failures to live up to his calling, but sets everything within the bigger context of God's grace and good purposes.

David should warn us against facile approval or disapproval of the people we come across. In a contemporary 'cancel culture', which tends to quickly evaluate people as a whole by particular things they say or do, we need scripture to remind us to keep our eyes open and our minds and hearts attentive to people as they really are.

FURTHER READING

John Goldingay, *The Theology of the Book of Samuel* (Cambridge University Press, 2024).

Robert P. Gordon, *1 & 2 Samuel: A commentary* (Paternoster, 1986).

Benjamin J.M. Johnson, *David: A man after God's own heart* (Cascade, 2021).

Matthew: forgiveness and reconciliation

Tim Welch

When I was training for Christian ministry, my senior pastor often used a phrase that has stayed with me over the years, that: 'The most beautiful word in the English language is "forgiveness".' While the experience of being forgiven is at the heart of the Christian gospel, the actual practice of accepting personal forgiveness or forgiving others can be much more challenging.

So, for the next two weeks we will explore aspects of forgiveness based on the teaching of Jesus from selected passages in Matthew's gospel. Praying the prayer Jesus taught his disciples, 'forgive us our debts, as we also have forgiven our debtors' (6:12), there is evidently an intrinsic link between our personal pattern of forgiveness and the received forgiveness of God. For, as Jesus amplifies, 'if you forgive others their trespasses, your heavenly Father will also forgive you' (6:14).

Given that Jesus teaches forgiveness and then later commissions his disciples to 'teach everything' that he has commanded them, with the promise that he is with them 'always, to the end of the age' (28:20), his 'disciples are to persist in a shared pursuit of obedience that is... propelled by a mutual commitment to forgiveness and reconciliation in Jesus' name' (Coutts, p. 137).

In a recent work, Kangil Kim employs the theological concept of *theosis*, considering this 'offers a hermeneutical key for understanding the embodied transformation of forgiveness in Matthew, namely our transformative participation in God's forgiving nature' (Kim, pp. 1–2). Consequently, as we will explore, the gospel according to Matthew calls for a knowledge and practice of forgiveness whereby, as disciples, we participate in the experience that 'God is with us' (1:23).

Bible quotations are taken from the NRSV. Author references are to works in the 'further reading' list.

1 Forgiveness is in the name

Matthew 1:18–25

Before we look at the teaching of Jesus about forgiveness, we do well to pause and consider Matthew's opening account as he introduces the birth (literally, 'genesis-origins') of Jesus the Messiah (1:1, 18). From the outset, Matthew's infancy narratives frame Jesus as the fulfilment of scripture anchored in the lineage of David, while also extending far beyond that genealogy. The supernatural conception of Jesus is attributed to the agency of the Holy Spirit (vv. 18, 20), as Joseph is drawn into the sequence of events surrounding the incarnation. Here, Joseph is reassured by the angel and instructed what to name the child, and the reason for this name: 'Jesus, for he will save his people from their sins' (v. 21).

In this first chapter, Matthew presents Jesus as the fulfilment of God's salvation drama, evident from Abraham to David, and then David to Jesus, culminating in the climactic arrival of 'the Messiah' (v. 16). All the messianic hopes of past centuries are met in Jesus Christ, the Anointed One, our Saviour.

Amid the complexity of Joseph's life and the predicament he finds himself in, Joseph is commended for being 'a righteous man' (v. 19). He wants to treat Mary, his betrothed, with gentleness and compassion, even though he had rights to publicly shame her. And yet in their circumstances, Joseph's acceptance of God's will and purposes is worked out, even above Joseph's own rights and honour.

Joseph and Mary surely discovered great strength and encouragement from the promise of the name 'Emmanuel', linked to their son Jesus. Here was the fulfilment of God's promise in Isaiah 7:14. Furthermore, here was great affirmation that Jesus is God-with-us. Indeed, saving people from their sins, by forgiveness, was at the very heart of Jesus' mission and ministry.

For Matthew's biography of Jesus, it seems particularly significant that God-with-us is so clearly announced at the start of the gospel, as well as encapsulated in the final words of Jesus, assuring disciples then and now that we need to remember the Saviour's promise, 'I am with you always, to the end of the age' (28:20).

Jesus is what Jesus does – he is Forgiver and Reconciler.

2 Family likenesses

Matthew 5:1–12

The wonder of the gospel is that we each come before God just as we are. Indeed, it is a truism that we can come no other way, and with that posture Jesus welcomes us as we are, today. Yet the kingdom teaching of Jesus from the mountainside (chapters 5—7), is quick to point out the higher ethical demands on all who will follow Jesus, both individually and corporately. Indeed, the variety of ethical lifestyle choices and devotional practices covered in the sermon on the mount assume engagement with real-life contexts and people, rather than a siloed spirituality.

Also, let's not miss the significant parallel between Moses delivering God's revelation on Mount Sinai (Exodus 19:3) with Jesus teaching his disciples on a mountain about how to live God's way with even greater potency, thus fulfilling both law and the prophets (Matthew 5:17–20). Mountains will feature again throughout this gospel as Jesus engages followers with significant insights into his divine power for healing (15:29–30), transfiguration and transformation (17:1–2) and ultimately for commission (28:16–20). At each of these junctures, the hearers are disciples and potential disciples who are considering the perfect righteousness of Jesus as both the example and provider of power to live out the beatitudes listed in our reading.

While the 'blessed are…' list offers rewards for the repentant (vv. 3–11), Keener observes how 'Matthew intends his audience to hear all the beatitudes together (his Gospel would have been read in church assemblies), not for them to be taken piecemeal' (Keener, p. 104). Consequent themes emerge, as the benefits of the coming kingdom of heaven are discovered by those who are 'poor in spirit', those who are repentant and 'mourn' about personal sin as well as too many who are broken by sin and injustice. The flow of these beatitudes leads to a meekness which is not ours naturally by right; rather, it's the family likeness of our Lord Jesus Christ working his power within everyone who believes in him.

Jesus then caps his kingdom manifesto with the call to be peacemakers, who 'will be called children of God' (v. 9). Let's consider if there are ways we can (re)discover Jesus-like qualities to pursue peace and reconciliation in our life today. These are to be our reflected characteristics and likenesses in the family of God.

3 Heart matters

Matthew 5:21–30

Jesus' 'kingdom of God' teaching challenges a response from every generation, getting to the heart of our private motivations and actions. Significantly, Jesus begins his ministry proclaiming that entrance to the kingdom of God is by repentance (4:17). Following Jesus is a costly business which will demand everything (8:18–22), including a deep inspection that warrants a root-and-branch check in areas highlighted in today's reading, namely anger and lust. Using illustrations which assume a connection between our relationship with God and how we treat others, the words of Jesus uncomfortably scrutinise the public and private condition of our heart and practice.

First, taking the scenario of murder (vv. 21–22), Jesus concurs with the commandment 'You shall not murder' (Exodus 20:13), yet disarms hearers by exposing the root cause of murder: if anyone is 'angry with a brother or sister, you will be liable to judgement' (v. 22). If feelings of anger at another person is reprehensible, there is greater harm still when anger is expressed in words of contempt, exampled by the insult 'Raca'/'you fool' (v. 22). Let's be honest, these are not easy considerations given our human propensity to hold and breed grudges with fiery critical thoughts of another. Left to fester, 'friendly fire' grievances can so easily boil over with insults, harsh words and the murderous thoughts that Jesus exposes.

Similarly, the realities of lust and adultery are also highlighted as danger zones that require ruthless elimination. Jesus' dramatic response (vv. 29–30) reveals how seriously God views sin, with a view of purity that pushes the red lines of appropriate behaviour back further to include affairs of the heart.

Although no human court would be able to consider a case of inward anger or thought-adultery, the solemn nature of Jesus' challenge makes us stop to consider the essentials of being reconciled to a brother or sister, before making an offering to God 'at the altar' (v. 23). The geographical implications implied here might require returning to the temple in Jerusalem before continuing in ministry, revealing acts of reconciliation require urgent, costly and decisive intervention.

Under the microscope of God's searching gaze, repentance is the radical means of changing our mind to be truly forgiven. Surely such matters of the heart equate to the final clause in this chapter, to 'be perfect, therefore, as your heavenly Father is perfect' (5:48), which thankfully is made possible by God's amazing grace.

4 Loving enemies

Matthew 5:38–48

The countercultural teaching of Jesus in the sermon on the mount continues to raise the bar in terms of our response to life's harshest challenges and injustices. Indeed, some of the horrors and evil experienced by too many in the world cry out for justice, as some have to take big decisions about whether to seek litigation or other appropriate action against aggressive evil enemy forces.

Of course, Jesus' words were addressed to hearers oppressed by political and religious powers and pushed around daily; they naturally wanted revenge, which would feel like justice. Everyday life seemed unfair, and the scenarios Jesus paints in these verses challenge the way we might think about personal insults (v. 39), being taken to court (v. 40), being exploited (v. 41), bombarded by requests to meet financial needs (v. 42) and knowing how to deal with personal enemies (v. 43). Hence, the words of Jesus require careful and personal interpretation. I recognise that humanly it will be impossible to love the 'enemy' who murdered your parent, or the 'enemy' who took your job unfairly or who made you bankrupt, or the 'enemy' who damaged your life all those years ago, etc. (the examples are far-reaching).

So, let's aim for the baseline here, that Jesus is encouraging hearers and readers to have a forgiving and generous heart with a 'righteousness [that] exceeds that of the Scribes and Pharisees' (5:20). If we are to be effective peacemakers, the Jesus way, then daily we need both the righteousness and the power of the One who would later say, 'Father, forgive them' (Luke 23:34).

Miroslav Volf faced this crisis between knowing about forgiveness and actually offering forgiveness, when, at the end of a lecture, Jürgen Moltmann stood and asked him, 'But can you embrace a *cětnik*?' – the 'enemy' who had killed so many of Volf's own people (Volf, p. 9). It seems appropriate to give Volf the final comment and challenge here:

'All sufferers can find comfort in the solidarity of the Crucified; but only those who struggle against evil by following the example of the Crucified will discover him at their side. To claim the comfort of the Crucified while rejecting his way is to advocate not only cheap grace but a deceitful ideology' (Volf, p. 24).

5 Mercy-full forgiveness

Matthew 6:5–15

In the fifth petition of the prayer Jesus taught his disciples, asking 'Our Father in heaven' to 'forgive us our debts, as we also have forgiven our debtors' (vv. 9, 12), an intrinsic link is established between God's mercy received and mercy demonstrated, which is to be the hallmark of everyone in Jesus' kingdom community. In the mercy-filled community Jesus is gathering, Jon Coutts comments: 'One cannot presume to be made right with God without seeking to be made right with other children of God that one has harmed' (p. 124).

Yet, as we noted in previous sections of the sermon on the mount, hidden issues of anger and lust ultimately destroy our relationships and need to be addressed and forgiven before we can truly worship God. Matthew predicates this on the relationship encapsulated in the way Jesus addresses his Father in heaven, inviting all to share this relational designation by praying: 'Our Father' (v. 9). The fact that Jesus specifies plurality in this tiny word 'our' reinforces the point that our praying is not just a private matter; rather, it is the work of the gathered fellowship or community, bound together to participate in the life of God the Father and God the Son.

While some commentators focus on Matthew's use of the word 'debts' in verse 12, contrasted with Luke's reference to 'sins' in the same prayer (Luke 11:4), the matter of reconciliation is far more important than mere semantics. Helpfully, the power of this prayer forces each of us to evaluate our personal debts or sins before the scorching scrutiny of 'Our Father in heaven', in ways that neither maximise the sins of others nor minimise our own debts. So, rather than our propensity to forgive others being a condition of God forgiving us, as some interpret the clause in verse 15, surely it is as we forgive those who sin against us, that we are actually invited to participate in the reason Jesus came, to 'save his people from their sins' (1:21).

Therefore, how we live life in the kingdom of God is far more than simply trying to imitate the reconciliatory pattern of Jesus. By praying the Lord's Prayer, our lived theology is to embody forgiveness, 'such that we participate in God's forgiving life' (Kim, pp. 29–30), which I like to think of as 'mercy-full' forgiveness (with the accent on God's fullness!).

6 Go and learn

Matthew 9:1–13

This section in Matthew 9 adds texture to the classic 'forgiveness' passages in Matthew's gospel, (already explored in 6:12–15, and to be covered next week in chapter 18). The narrative of forgiveness and healings in homes in Capernaum (see also 8:5–17), point to Jesus being 'God with us' (1:23). Indeed, forgiveness, healing and restoration are all integral to the power of Jesus to reconcile people to God as well as with one another. This is powerfully evidenced by the authority Jesus exerts to enable both the miracle of forgiveness and healing for the paralysed man (v. 6), as well as restored relationships with God and others as they sit down at the table to eat together (v. 10).

Noting how debilitating paralysis isolates and restricts the whole body, the power of Jesus applies healing and reconciliation to fractures caused by the destructive power of sin. The healing of the paralysed man, combined with Jesus then having dinner at Matthew's house, along with 'many tax collectors and sinners' (v. 10), shines a spotlight on the redemptive and transformative forgiving power of God now available on earth. As 'God with us,' Jesus liberates people who were culturally ostracised and rejected and he rehabilitates them together as a restored community of sick and sinful people. According to the proclamation of Jesus, 'Those who are well have no need of a physician, but those who are sick' (v. 12), and Matthew and other unthinkable characters are then invited to a place at the table to enjoy fellowship, enacting and experiencing the forgiveness and acceptance of Jesus. How typical of Jesus to unite those who are previously broken and divided.

Finally, let's zoom into the brief sentence Jesus then speaks, 'Go and learn what this means' (v. 13). Of course, the ultimate supreme power and authority to forgive sins belongs to Jesus alone, but that said, here Jesus is teaching would-be followers that God was also giving 'such authority to human beings' (v. 8). As part of their discipleship training school with Jesus, the power of God will soon be evident in the commission of the twelve, who are given 'authority over unclean spirits, to cast them out, and to cure every disease and every sickness' (10:1), and later to 'forgive sins' as part and parcel of the healing work of Jesus (18:18–20). It is time to go and learn!

Guidelines

The kingdom teaching of Jesus around forgiveness and reconciliation in Matthew's gospel is alarmingly simple and yet profoundly personal and challenging. Again, it is important to recognise that much sin and conflict have involved unimaginable pain and heartache, and for some healing and wholeness may seem impossible right now. The violence and degradation experienced may have been so damaging that a much slower and carefully supervised pastoral and professional response will be necessary to assist the journey to recovery. And so, we pray for the healing and restoration of many who are suffering the consequences of evil perpetrators, that all victims will detect hope this day.

For some of us, perhaps we need to audit our responses to themes covered this past week, considering how we respond to aspects such as: the beautiful name of Jesus: 'Saviour'; the call to be merciful and peacemakers; any latent anger and/or lust within our own heart; our secret list of 'enemies' or those people we actively try to avoid; the call of Jesus to learn, embody and practise God's forgiving power.

The Christian church is called to serve Christ in the power of Christ, joining God's work of healing in a broken world. Perhaps it will be helpful to pray the Litany of Reconciliation from Coventry Cathedral:

The hatred which divides nation from nation, race from race, class from class. **Father, Forgive.**
The covetous desires of people and nations to possess what is not their own. **Father, Forgive.**
The greed which exploits the work of human hands and lays waste the earth. **Father, Forgive.**
Our envy of the welfare and happiness of others. **Father, Forgive.**
Our indifference to the plight of the imprisoned, the homeless, the refugee. **Father, Forgive.**
The lust which dishonours the bodies of men, women and children. **Father, Forgive.**
The pride which leads us to trust ourselves and not in God. **Father, Forgive.**
Be kind to one another, tender hearted, forgiving one another, as God in Christ forgave you. **Amen.**

coventrycathedral.org.uk/reconciliation/reconciliation-ministry/litany-of-reconciliation

1 Keys to the kingdom

Matthew 16:13–28

In today's intriguing passage in which Jesus commissions Simon Peter, we note the first use of the word 'church' (*ekklesia*, v. 18) as the gathering of Christ's new community, with instructions and a promise (reinforced in 18:18) that 'whatever you bind on earth will be bound in heaven, and whatever you loose on earth will be loosed in heaven' (v. 19). Jesus explains that Peter has received his insights about Jesus' identity from the Father in heaven, rather than 'flesh and blood' (v. 17). Ownership of the keys of the kingdom of heaven are handed from Jesus to Peter, signifying the delegated authority of the one holding them. Significantly for all disciples, that same authority is then extended plurally to all disciples in chapter 18, within the context of enabling forgiveness and reconciliation in the church. Such 'key-holders' are given an assurance that Jesus promises, them and us, that he 'will build his church, and the gates of Hades will not prevail against it' (v. 18). Forgiveness is to be central to God's community.

The nature of keys for 'opening' and powers for 'binding' and 'loosing' has provoked much discussion in commentaries. However, the relevance of today's reading to the practice of forgiveness (to be developed in chapter 18) highlights a clear basis for Christians in every culture and generation.

Peter's confession of faith that Jesus is the 'Messiah, the Son of the living God' (v. 16) recognises that the source of all future authority is divine. Such a revelation changes everything for Simon, who is given a name-change to Peter, or 'Rocky' (according to Keener, p. 271), with all the association of the wise builder building on rock, who hears the words of Jesus and believes them as foundational for life and ministry (7:24–25; see also 1 Corinthians 3:11).

As Peter employs the rock metaphor in his later letter, the church as God's new community can only be built with Christ as the cornerstone (1 Peter 2:4–8). Peter and all Jesus-disciples are living stones, built together around the same declaration of faith that Peter so clearly articulated in Caesarea Philippi. Indeed, Peter still had much to learn about forgiving others and options to bind or loose, arguably referring to the practice of forgiveness in the community of the church (see also John 20:22–23). I wonder about the impact if we remember we also have this set of divine 'keys' available to us today?

2 The posture of forgiveness

Matthew 18:1–14

The repetition of the 'binding' and 'loosing' teaching of Jesus in verses 18–20 'epitomizes the transformative dynamics of heaven and earth in Matthew, God and the human revealed in our practice of forgiveness and prayer' (Kim, p. 83). It is helpful to note how these emphases are situated within a chapter where Jesus calls for all members of God's community to 'change and become like children' (v. 3). Given a child in the ancient world implied a lack of identity, status or respect, Jesus elevates the notion of being childlike as the entry requirement for the kingdom of heaven. In the estimation of Jesus, this is true greatness, which suggests several core postures for a discipleship of forgiveness and reconciliation.

First, the 'Welcome Posture' (v. 5), which challenges how we are to treat brothers and sisters in the family of God, given our human response will reflect how we treat Christ himself. This salutary reminder causes me to pause before dismissing the 'other' person who has disagreed with me or challenged my position or power, etc. Indeed, verse 5 prompts us to recognise Jesus in the 'other'. Thinking how quickly children in the school playground generally manage to sort out their squabbles and fights and move on, I wonder if Jesus was hoping for something similar in his family.

Added to this is the 'Protection Posture' built into Jesus' teaching here (vv. 6–9), which highlights how we have the potential to be a 'stumbling block' to others. Our shared weakness as 'little ones' encourages us to avoid tripping 'others' up by any sinful actions or words which will wreak havoc. Instead, we are to be 'stepping stones' for others, rather than the 'stumbling blocks' that incur God's judgement.

Finally, the 'Pastoral Posture' is noted (vv. 10–14), where the impetus called for is to go after the 'one' who has wandered off. Whether this one is the weakest, the lost or even the disagreeable 'other', God's love longs for any wandering person to be reunited with the other ninety-nine, thus reestablishing unity.

So, let's absorb this thrust of Jesus teaching his disciples how life in the kingdom of heaven is to be reflected on earth. For them and us, as peacemakers we are to learn to handle conflict by integrating the three postures highlighted above: Welcoming, Protecting and Pastoral.

3 The forgiving church

Matthew 18:15–20

Having announced the formation of the church in 16:18, Jesus is now setting out ground rules for any gathering to emulate forgiveness patterns which will be the hallmark of God's new community. It is striking to observe the realistic and practical teaching of Jesus here, which again connects the dynamic life of heaven on earth.

Perhaps it is strangely reassuring that Jesus assumes the church will face relational problems. Here, the great promise of God is issued, that 'where two or three are gathered in my name, I am there among them' (v. 20). This is Jesus, 'God with us' (1:23), promising all the presence and fullness of the Godhead; but not to boost morale when a prayer meeting has a disappointing attendance (as sometimes misappropriated!), rather it's actually the promise of God's presence for all situations where reconciliation is required.

The practical measures Jesus teaches involve a process which turns to face the sin or problem issue directly (v. 15). Sin is serious before God and must not be ignored. While interpretations of this passage sometimes rush to create arguments for excommunication, it is important to note that there are significant earlier stages to navigate before any drastic disciplinary measures are taken. Thankfully, these early steps of practical teaching have all the pastoral assurances of Christ's risen presence and compassion:

Step 1: 'Go and point out the fault when the two of you are alone' (v. 15). This enables space to create a healthy listening environment where problematic issues can, hopefully, be dealt with personally and quietly.

Step 2: If good listening is not achieved, then Jesus provides a model facilitation process, involving witnesses and, only then, a widening circle, presumably to be handled with great pastoral sensitivity (vv. 16–17). The earlier verses about compassionately seeking a 'wandering sheep' (vv. 12–13) are applicable here.

Step 3: If listening fails and unrepentance persists, the matter is then to be taken to the church with the assurance of God's continuing presence. While church history records some appalling acts of discipline and shunning, the rationale of Jesus here is that any final step should treat the guilty party as a pagan or tax collector (v. 17). Those connotations in the gospels remind us that Jesus was a friend of sinners, engaging with tax collectors and Gentiles, and One who takes the initiative towards all who are lost. In the footsteps of Jesus, we follow.

4 The seventy-seven times pattern

Matthew 18:21–22

I'm interested that it is Matthew recording this conversation between Simon Peter and Jesus, given Matthew's own development of this theme of forgiveness in his gospel. Last week we looked at the teaching of Jesus that asks God to 'forgive us our debts, as we also have forgiven our debtors' (6:12). Now in chapter 18, Peter is testing Jesus' teaching to see where the red lines and limits for this revolutionary practice of forgiveness are: 'Lord, if my brother or sister sins against me, how often should I forgive? As many as seven times?' (18:21).

The fact that both Peter and Matthew are part of the first church raises significant relational dynamics which are probably applicable in any local church. Peter, the self-employed fisherman, had spent a lifetime loathing tax collectors such as Matthew, and for good reason. Debt collection on behalf of the Romans enabled Matthew and colleagues to employ a raft of dodgy deals and despicable exploitation. Here you can almost sense Peter's deeply held prejudices against Matthew (and probably others) coming to mind, given who they are and what they have done. No wonder Peter wants to know the cut-off line for forgiveness, probably drawing on some existing rabbinic traditions which factored in limitations of repeat-forgiveness for the same sin (Coutts, p. 128).

Jesus' response that 'seventy-seven times' forgiveness is expected, and not just 'seven times', opens a pattern of forgiveness which does not permit counting or keeping a record of wrongs (see also 1 Corinthians 13:5). This illuminates the earlier teaching of Jesus further, that 'if you forgive others their trespasses, your heavenly Father will also forgive you; but if you do not forgive others, neither will your Father forgive your trespasses' (6:14–15). While that implied a conditional element to receiving forgiveness, the 'seventy-seven times' quota oils the covenantal life of all Christian communities given forgiveness is now framed around 'reciprocity' (Coutts, p.128).

Practically, this may be a hard, even painful, teaching to apply in our personal situations. But Jesus is teaching a supernatural mercy that looks at another offender based on the divine grace we ourselves have received. So, as unlikely as it may seem, Peter and Matthew could know reconciliation the Jesus way. And surely that also offers us hope for fractured relationships to be tackled by means of the 'seventy-seven times' pattern.

5 To forgive, or not to forgive; that is the question

Matthew 18:21–35

'Reordering our desires' is how Helen Paynter entitles her penultimate chapter in *Blessed Are the Peacemakers* (Paynter, pp. 320–326), arguing that 'if we are honest, the tendency to view violence as "other people's problem" lies within us all' (Paynter, p. 320). Paynter warns of the danger that a 'plank' can so easily exist in our own eyes, which makes reorientation before God so vital 'to protect us from the pride and arrogance of the servant who chased down his friend for a small debt when he had been forgiven an enormous one' (pp. 320, 324).

Indeed, the story Jesus tells here about this unmerciful servant offers a profoundly uncomfortable and compelling challenge: to forgive, or not to forgive. Responding to Peter's question about the extent forgiveness will be expected, Jesus reverses Lamech's revenge in Genesis 4:24 to state a principle of unlimited forgiveness based on the generosity of God.

Our human propensity for inconsistent patterns of forgiveness is exposed when we enjoy the sense of God's forgiveness personally, while being less than generous with forgiveness for others who have angered or annoyed us. Reflecting personally, even though I like to think of myself as a steady and generally peaceable character, I recognise how easily one can build an internal case against others who I consider have 'sinned against me', with issues that range from trivial to highly significant.

Rather than responding with the direct and transparent conversational approach advised by Jesus (18:15), it's so easy to hold on to resentments and hostile feelings. Hence the call to regularly reorder our desires before God, by taking stock of our outstanding 'debts' and checking if we are unwittingly playing the role of the unmerciful servant, however legitimate and justifiable we may think our claim is. As many know from personal experience and too many sleepless nights, such grudges are always destructive.

Tom Wright's advice to all strugglers in this area is helpful. It 'is not that one should therefore swallow all resentment and "forgive and forget" as though nothing had happened. The key thing is that one should never, ever give up making forgiveness and reconciliation one's goal. If confrontation has to happen, as it often does, it must always be with forgiveness in mind, never revenge' (Wright, p. 39).

6 Extravagant forgiveness straight from the heart

Matthew 26:6–30

As our explorations of forgiveness and reconciliation culminates in the suffering and death of Jesus, the focus today is on the assurance expressed in the last supper, as Jesus gathers around the table with his disciples and takes a cup saying: 'Drink from it, all of you, for this is my blood of the covenant, which is poured out for many for the forgiveness of sins' (vv. 27–28). This is a significant bookending in Matthew's account, given Jesus was introduced at birth as the one who 'will save his people from their sins' (1:21).

Indeed, Jesus has regularly expressed forgiveness to both Jews and Gentiles in the many 'meal' encounters he has with 'sinners' and 'tax collectors' (see other examples in Matthew 9:9–13; 11:19; 14:14–21; 15:32–28).

Then, prior to the last supper, Matthew contrasts two human hearts: a woman's extravagant and sacrificial anointing of Jesus with Judas' deceitful and self-serving betrayal of Jesus. Though an outsider, the woman is publicly demonstrating her lavish love and appreciation to Jesus by anointing him with expensive perfume in a beautiful act of worship. Conversely, Judas is acting secretively and out of selfish concern for what he can gain financially from a despicable act of betrayal in collusion with the chief priests. Yet, even at the table, Judas is invited to drink from the cup. The commentary Jesus offers elsewhere, following a similar act of generous devotion, gives insight to their contrasting heart conditions: 'I tell you, her many sins have been forgiven; hence she has shown great love. But the one to whom little is forgiven loves little' (Luke 7:47).

For us, this is a timely reminder for our participation at the Lord's table, that this simple meal offers a welcome for all sinners saved by God's grace. Table fellowship rightly has deeply personal meaning regarding the forgiveness of our own sins; but the table is also open to others who are equally welcomed by Jesus. No wonder serious reminders are in order that we should examine our own hearts first before eating the bread and drinking the cup together (1 Corinthians 11:28). It is at the table we remember, and in Jesus we are re-membered, together, as a forgiven and reconciled people.

Guidelines

Matthew concludes his gospel with the great commission, as Jesus instructs his disciples to teach disciples 'to obey everything that I have commanded you. And remember, I am with you always, to the end of the age' (28:20).

The focus of this application is on the teaching we (may) have received regarding forgiveness and reconciliation, and considering the extent we are actively 'teaching' and helping others to obey everything Jesus has commanded within this vital area of discipleship. To aid your reflections, you might like to consider these questions and a suggested exercise:

- Whose example of practical forgiveness and reconciliation has inspired me, and what are the core features of their story?
- How am I, or my church, matching up to being a forgiving church, in ways explored over the past week (especially Matthew 18)?

An exercise: Draw a circle to represent a table where Jesus sits to share bread and the cup with a group of friends. Indicate the seat belonging to Jesus and the seat for you. Then add to the seating plan the names or initials of others who have caused (or are causing) you pain or broken relationship. Prayerfully imagine Jesus offering the cup of forgiveness to them and to you, while speaking out the words of Jesus in Matthew 6:9–15. Finally, be quiet as you sense Jesus saying to each person individually around the table: 'Take heart, child; your sins are forgiven' (9:2). As you are enabled, pray God's blessing on each person on your list.

FURTHER READING

Jon Coutts, 'Jesus as a teacher of forgiveness' in Charles L. Quarles and Charles Nathan Ridlehoover (eds), *Jesus as Teacher in the Gospel of Matthew* (T&T Clark, 2025), pp. 123–137.

Kangil Kim, *Theosis and Forgiveness in the Gospel of Matthew* (Fortress Academic, 2024).

Craig S. Keener, *Matthew* (IVP, 1997).

Helen Paynter, *Blessed Are the Peacemakers* (Zondervan Academic, 2023).

Miroslav Volf, *Exclusion and Embrace: Theological exploration of identity, otherness and reconciliation* (Abingdon, 1996).

Tom Wright, *Matthew for Everyone* (SPCK, 2002).

Ezra

Miriam Bier Hinksman

Ezra and Nehemiah traditionally belong together as one book, telling the story of the return of the Judahite exiles from Babylon to Jerusalem under the Persian empire. The story is told thematically rather than strictly chronologically, with narrative material interspersed with letters, genealogies, first-person memoirs and prayers, to show how the returned exiles begin to rebuild and re-establish their identity as the people of God. Ezra is concerned with rebuilding the *house of God* (Ezra 1—6) and reestablishing the *word of God* (Ezra 7—10). Nehemiah is concerned with rebuilding the walls of the *city of God* (Nehemiah 1—7) and re-establishing the *covenant community of God* (Nehemiah 8—13).

For the next two weeks we focus on the two movements in Ezra – the move to rebuild the temple (Ezra 1—6, from 539BC) and the move to re-establish the Torah (Ezra 7—10, from 458BC). By the end of Ezra, the second temple is complete, and the postexilic people of God are defined as a people for worship and a people of the book, with temple and Torah established as key features of second-temple Judaism.

Crucially, though, in Ezra the people of God are those who have been forged in the fire of the Babylonian exile. On return to Jerusalem, there are major concerns for the continuity and survival of the people of God, and for maintaining their distinctive identity. Ezra reaches into the past to establish links with the pre-exilic people of God, giving increasing weight to written records and documents that prove continuity with the past. He then draws a firm boundary around the community of returned exiles as the 'remnant' who should now be considered the 'true Israel'. As we shall see, this leads to some thorny problems, as the community attempt to determine who belongs and who does not.

Unless otherwise stated, Bible quotations are taken from the NRSV.

1 'Everyone whose spirit God had stirred'

Ezra 1

The book of Ezra begins with King Cyrus of Persia's edict that the Judahite exiles in Babylon may 'go up to Jerusalem in Judah and rebuild the house of the Lord, the God of Israel' (v. 3; compare 2 Chronicles 36:22–23). This marks a crucial point in the history of the people of God – the point at which the Babylonian exile ends, and the 'second temple' period begins (539BC).

Under the Babylonian empire, some of Judah's key leaders (including the king, Jehoiachin) had been deported to Babylon (597BC). Then the city and temple of Jerusalem fell to Babylon (587BC), and even more of the great and the good were exiled, leaving the temple desecrated and the city in ruins. There had been big questions as to how and why this could have happened. There had been difficult answers to face, concerning sin, punishment and what it truly meant to be the people of God. But there had also been prophetic hope, that exile would not be the end for God's people and that, somehow, a remnant would be restored to the land.

Now, with Cyrus' decree, that restoration begins. This is not, however, primarily of Cyrus' own making. Rather, it is because the God of heaven acts decisively in history on behalf of God's people. God 'stirs up' Cyrus' spirit, not only to release the exiles, but also to return the treasures that had been taken as plunder from the first temple (vv. 1, 7).

In response to Cyrus' decree, 'everyone whose spirit God had stirred got ready to go up and rebuild the house of the Lord in Jerusalem' (v. 5). This is not yet a wholesale return of all the Judahites living in Babylon, just as the exile itself was not a wholesale deportation of all the people of Judah (many of the poor of the land stayed behind). But with this return, we can observe three developing themes. First, God is sovereign, even over foreign rulers, and can use them to advance the cause of God's people. Second, the purpose of the return is first and foremost to rebuild the house of the Lord in Jerusalem. Third, the identity of the people of God as 'the exiles' (v. 11) begins to emerge.

2 'Now these were the people'

Ezra 2

A genealogical record is not always the most exciting reading. Rather than reading Ezra 2 from start to finish, then, as though it were a story, we will instead take particular notice of the way the lists are framed and how each group of people is identified. Verse 1 presents what follows as a record of 'the people of the province who came from those captive exiles who King Nebuchadnezzar of Babylon had carried captive to Babylon' (v. 1). The last verse of the chapter affirms that it is *these* people – the ones who have returned from exile – who comprise 'all Israel in their towns' (v. 70).

Of course, time has passed, so those recorded here are not necessarily those who had been taken into exile themselves, but rather their children and grandchildren. However, clear links with the past are established. Zerubbabel and Jeshua are first in the list of leaders in verse 2. Zerubbabel was King Jehoiachin's grandson in the line of David and Jeshua was from a priestly family in the line of Aaron. As governor of the Persian province of Yehud (i.e. Judah), and high priest in the second temple, respectively, Zerubbabel and Jeshua provide continuity with the political and religious leadership of pre-exilic Judah.

The next groups of people are those who are identified by a significant male ancestor (vv. 3–20) and those who trace their lineage to an ancestral town (vv. 21–35). There are also those who are identified by their ancestors' role in the first temple, as priests, Levites, singers, gatekeepers and servants (vv. 35–58).

Then there are some who are identified by their Babylonian town, who 'could not prove their families or their descent, whether they belonged to Israel' (vv. 59–60); as well as priests who could not prove their ancestry, who were forbidden from serving in the new temple (vv. 61–63). We see, here, the turn to written records to establish continuity with the past, and the desire to draw a clear boundary around those who belong.

When the assembly arrives in Jerusalem, the first thing that happens is that freewill offerings are made so that the temple can be rebuilt (vv. 68–69). The people of God are a people for worship, and they have come back to Jerusalem to rebuild the house of God.

3 'The peoples of the lands'

Ezra 3

Once the Israelites are settled in their towns, the altar is set up so that worship can resume even before the temple itself is completed. Another reason given for restoring the altar, though, is 'because they were in dread of the people of the lands' (v. 3). The tension between these 'people of the lands' and the returned exiles is a key issue throughout book of Ezra.

So who are these 'people of the lands'? It is very likely they comprise native Judahites who had not been taken into exile, as well as Samarians, moved in from the north under the Assyrians after the fall of Samaria in 722BC, and others from the surrounding lands who would have had different religions and different gods. This mixing of peoples and gods is seen as a threat to the purity and identity of the returned exiles, who had 'retained their ethnic and cultural identity throughout the exile' and who now identified religious pluralism and idolatry as part of the reason why the exile had happened (Harrington, p. 42).

Laying the foundations of the temple is thus the preserve of 'the priests and the Levites and *all who had come to Jerusalem from the captivity*' (v. 8, italics mine). Once the foundation is laid, there is an outpouring of praise. The work is not complete, but it is begun, and this is a sign of God's steadfast love for Israel. As well as shouts of joy, though, though there are tears from those among the returned exiles who are old enough to remember the first temple. We are not told why they are weeping, but the sounds of shouting and weeping commingle so that they cannot be distinguished. This is, perhaps, a good reminder to those in church leadership that occasions of praise and celebration for many in the congregation (for example, Christmas or Mothering Sunday) may at the same time be occasions of weeping for others.

4 'No part with us'

Ezra 4

Ezra 4 begins by recounting an altercation between Zerubbabel and a group described as the 'adversaries of Judah and Benjamin' (v. 1). This group trace their occupancy of the land back to King Esar-haddon of Assyria (681–669BC), and, they say, worship God just as the returned exiles do. Part of the Assyrians' strategy for keeping conquered peoples under control was mixing them up and relocating them. Peoples who were deported to other areas took their gods and religious practices with them. Although these 'adversaries' may well have worshipped the God of Israel, they likely worshipped other gods as well, and now they want to join in with Zerubbabel and the returned exiles in rebuilding the temple.

When they approach Zerubbabel, he draws a line between the returned exiles and these others, declaring that they 'shall have no part with us' in building a house for God (v. 3). Rejection leads to opposition, and the rebuffed adversaries, or 'people of the land', frustrate the plans of the returned exiles to the point that they are afraid to keep building (v. 4).

We see, now, how material from different timelines comes together to make a thematic point. After the work stopped, in verse 4, the narrative introduces two more instances of opposition putting a stop to the returned exiles' rebuilding efforts. First, there is a brief mention of an accusation made under Ahasuerus (485–465BC, v. 6). Second, there is a record of letters (in Aramaic) between Samarian opponents of building work in Jerusalem, and Artaxerxes (465–424BC; vv. 7–23). Both these instances come from later times, but they are included here and contribute to the theme of opposition to the building work.

The return and rebuilding were decreed by the Persian ruler under the sovereignty of God. It was begun with good intent by people who were totally committed and gave generously to make it happen. *But there are still difficulties along the way.* God is sovereign, but there are still challenges, and embedding two more episodes of opposition in the narrative here makes that point abundantly clear. The chapter finishes by returning to the situation in verse 4, stating that the 'work on the house of God in Jerusalem stopped and was discontinued' until the reign of Darius (521–486BC, v. 24).

5 'The prophets of God, helping them'

Ezra 5

At the end of Ezra 4, work on the house of God in Jerusalem had stopped. Ezra 5 resumes the story when the building work resumes, in the second year of Darius (about 15 years later). Work stopped because of opposition from adversaries and the people of the land. How did it get started again?

This is where the prophets Haggai and Zechariah come in. Reading the prophetic books that bear their names can help us understand a little more of the situation in Judah at that time. Haggai is direct and to the point. Although the work stopped because of opposition, Haggai thinks there is something else going on too – something to do with people being more interested in feathering their own nests than in continuing to rebuild the house of God (Haggai 1:9). Haggai points to the challenging circumstances facing the returned exiles, drought and economic hardship, and intimates that these difficulties are a direct result of their failing to prioritise God's house over their own homes.

Zechariah is more expansive and perhaps more encouraging to a people who are struggling. He brings the much-needed assurance that God is with them, and that God will see to it that the work is done (Zechariah 6:6). Together, Haggai and Zechariah provide the prophetic wake-up call that is needed for work on the house of God to begin again.

Building projects, however, rarely go smoothly. This time the project comes to the attention of Tattenai, the governor of the province Beyond-the-River (a large administrative area of the Persian Empire, of which the smaller province of Yehud was part). Tattenai questions the builders and writes to the king requesting further information to verify what they have told him – that Cyrus decreed that the house of God in Jerusalem should be rebuilt, and returned the gold and silver temple vessels that had been plundered from the first temple.

The importance of the written word comes to the fore again, as Tattenai writes and asks the king to search the annals and archives to find written evidence of the Judahites' claims. This insistence on returning to the written record will ultimately work in the returned exiles' favour.

6 Through prophecy, by command and decree

Ezra 6

In Ezra 6, Darius rediscovers Cyrus' edict (vv. 1–6) and instructs Tattenai to let the work on the house of God continue. He decrees that the cost of building is to be covered from the taxes and revenues raised in the province – that is to say, out of his own pocket. Everything needed for the daily sacrifices is also to be provided. There is an element of self-interest here – he asks for prayers for himself and his family – but it is still extraordinary that he not only endorses the rebuilding of the temple but pays for it himself. Remember, though, who is behind all this. Everything comes about 'by command of the God of Israel' (v. 14) who can 'turn the heart' of rulers towards God's people to accomplish God's purposes (v. 22). Thus the temple is completed – through prophecy, by God's command, and by royal decree (v. 14).

The temple is dedicated with joy and with sacrifice, including twelve male goats, representing the twelve original tribes of Israel, as a sin offering 'for all Israel' – where 'all Israel' is now defined in terms of 'the priests and the Levites, and the rest of the *returned exiles*' (v. 16, italics mine). Emphasis on 'the returned exiles' continues at the Passover celebrations (vv. 19–21). The people of God trace their identity back to the exodus as they celebrate the Passover, commemorating their release from slavery. But they now also identify themselves as those who have made a second exodus, from exile in the land of Babylon.

Notice, though, that the Passover meal is shared with 'all who had joined them and separated themselves from the pollutions of the nations of the land to seek the Lord, the God of Israel' (v. 21). So far in Ezra, there has been suspicion of anyone who claimed to worship God but hadn't gone into exile. Why are these others allowed to join in now?

There is no simple answer, but this inclusion introduces a note of ambiguity into what has, until now, been becoming a very exclusive definition of the people of God. It should perhaps give us pause as well, if there are those whose Christian credentials we might be dubious about, or whom we fear may even be a threat to the life and identity of the Christian community. When it comes to worship, is there a way for us to coexist such that all who seek forgiveness of sin, and desire to worship the Lord, may join in?

Guidelines

One of the major questions explored in Ezra is 'who are the people of God?' We see this question being worked out in the context of the return from Babylonian exile, when the continuity, identity and survival of God's people were at stake. In Ezra 1—6 the people of God are a people for worship. The purpose of the return from exile is to 'build God a house at Jerusalem' (1:2). As soon as the returned exiles arrive, they give offerings so that the building work can begin (2:68–69). Even before the rebuilding begins, the altar is restored and sacrificial worship resumes (3:3). The temple foundation is laid to great fanfare (3:10), and when opposition and discouragement come (as they always do, 4:4–5), prophetic voices spur the people on (5:1) until finally the temple is completed and dedicated (6:14–16). Sacrifices are offered (6:17) and the Passover is celebrated (6:19–22).

The people of God are also a people of the book, and this will take centre stage next week, when Ezra the scribe returns to Jerusalem to teach the Torah to the returned exiles. It is becoming increasingly evident, though, that in Ezra, the people of God are being defined as those who have returned from exile.

- How would you answer the question 'who are the people of God?'
- To what extent are the people of God still a people for worship?
- What does the building in which you worship say about the priority given by your local congregation to being a people for worship?

One of the overarching themes in Ezra is the sovereignty of God. Powerful people come and go, but God is able to 'stir up' these powerful people to accomplish God's own purposes for God's people.

- Can you see God at work in and through the powerful people in our world?
- Where (in the world, your local community, the church, your home or your own life) do you need to be reminded that God is sovereign and acts on behalf of those who are God's?

1 Ezra the scribe

Ezra 7

About 50 years after the temple is completed (516BC), there is another wave of migration, as a further group of exiles return to Jerusalem during the reign of King Artaxerxes (465–424 BC). With this group is Ezra himself, who has not yet appeared in the book. Ezra is introduced as a priest, a scribe and a scholar, who had 'set his heart to study the law of the Lord and to do it and to teach' (v. 10). His heart was to ensure the law of the Lord was re-established among the community of returned exiles in Jerusalem. In a pattern seen in previous chapters, Ezra has royal authorisation and funding for his mission.

Ezra 7 incorporates a letter from King Artaxerxes (in Aramaic) before changing to a first-person account of the return from verse 27 (the 'Ezra memoir'). Ezra's letter of endorsement from Artaxerxes has two main concerns: the *house* of God (vv. 15, 16, 17, 19, 20, 23, 24); and the *law* of God (vv. 11, 12, 14, 21, 25, 26). The house of God was the priority for the first group of returned exiles in Ezra 1—6. Now there is a complementary emphasis on the law of God, which is Ezra's particular expertise as a scribe 'skilled in the law of Moses' (v. 6). Ezra is charged by the Persian king to take people, money and temple vessels to Jerusalem, to ensure the work of the house of God is being fulfilled, but *also* to teach and judge the people according to the law of God (as well as the laws of the Persian king).

Ezra's return to Jerusalem is decreed by Artaxerxes, and he has royal backing and funding for his task. Ultimately, however, as with the first return, it all comes about because the king of heaven 'put such a thing as this into the heart of the king' (v. 27). God is sovereign. Ezra's journey succeeds not because of Artaxerxes' backing but because of God's steadfast love (v. 28) and because the 'gracious hand of his God was upon him' (v. 9; compare vv. 6, 28).

2 Preparations for the journey

Ezra 8:1–23

Ezra gathers all who are to go up to Jerusalem with him, about 2,000–5,000 in all (only the males are counted in the genealogical records in verses 1–14, but there would have been women and children as well). He then discovers that there are no Levites among the company. There are priests to serve in the temple, and temple treasures and vessels aplenty – but no Levites, who were responsible for some of the tasks enabling the day to day running of temple worship. This is a problem, because Ezra is charged with ensuring everything is happening as it should be in the house of God in Jerusalem. To do that, he needs Levites.

Ezra therefore gathers a team of eleven others (which with him makes twelve, the same as the number of tribes of Israel). Some of them are 'leaders' and others are 'wise', and he sends them to a place called Casiphia, to ask for 'ministers for the house of our God' (vv. 16–18). It is unclear what kind of a place Casiphia is, but evidently Ezra knows that there will be Levites there and his team returns with 38 Levites and 220 temple servants. The success of the request is once again attributed to 'the gracious hand of our God' (v. 18)

As the people prepare to leave, Ezra proclaims a fast, to seek God and pray for safe passage (vv. 21–23). Some of us still pray for 'travelling mercies' even today, but Ezra's phrasing is especially telling. He seeks a 'safe journey' – more literally, a 'straight way,' calling to mind the prophet Isaiah's proclamation of return in Isaiah 40:3.

There is a contrast, here, between Ezra's approach to seeking a safe journey and Nehemiah's. Both fast and pray, but Ezra does not feel that he can ask the king for protection because he has spoken so confidently about *God's* protection – that 'gracious hand' again (v. 22). Nehemiah, on the other hand, asks the king for letters of guarantee and is also given an armed guard (Nehemiah 2:7–9). *Both* men are confident that God's hand is upon them and their journey – but Ezra leaves it all up to God, whereas Nehemiah also calls upon human assistance. Ultimately, though, both men attribute their safe arrival in Jerusalem to God.

3 Set apart and holy

Ezra 8:24–36

Ezra's final preparation is to 'set apart' twelve priests to take responsibility for the extraordinary amount of silver and gold that has been given for the house of God, as well as the temple vessels. Everything is carefully recorded and weighed out to the priests. There is a commission, or consecration, of sorts, as Ezra hands over the responsibility for bearing these treasures to Jerusalem to the twelve priests. They are 'holy to the Lord', just as the vessels for which they are now responsible are 'holy'; and the free-will offerings they carry are for the Lord, 'the God of your ancestors' (v. 28). Here we see the concern for establishing continuity with the past alongside the identification of those who returned from exile with the twelve tribes of Israel of old. There are twelve priests who are 'holy to the Lord', just as there were twelve tribes of Israel, who were set apart and chosen from all the nations to be holy to the Lord (Deuteronomy 7:6; 14:2).

Ezra records the date of departure, but of the journey itself all that is said is that 'the hand of our God was upon us', so that despite the threats of enemy and ambush, they arrive safely in Jerusalem (v. 31). The gold and silver and temple vessels are handed over to the priests in the house of God, and once everything has been safely delivered and carefully recorded, the people turn to worship. The sacrifices that follow again make the point that 'those who had come from captivity, the returned exiles' should now be considered the true Israel, with twelve bulls offered for 'all Israel' and twelve male goats for a sin offering (v. 35) representing the twelve tribes of Israel.

Finally, after worship and sacrifice have been offered on behalf of 'all Israel', the king's commissions to the regional leaders are also delivered (v. 36). Just as God is the sovereign mover, who first stirs the heart of the Persian king towards the people of God, so too must the people of God's priority be the God of heaven. We would do well to remember this too: worship the God of heaven, *then* carry out your responsibilities to human powers – in that order.

4 Faithlessness and abominations

Ezra 9

The remainder of Ezra deals with an issue that, in Ezra's view, threatens the very survival of the people of God: marriage between the returned exiles and the 'peoples of the lands' (vv. 1–4). We have seen how, in Ezra, a case is building for understanding the returned exiles as 'true Israel' over against 'the peoples of the land', even when some of those peoples were worshippers of God or also had a Hebrew heritage. Now the 'peoples of the lands' are equated with the ancient Canaanites, Hittites, Perizzites, Jebusites and Amorites, recalling the instructions in Deuteronomy 7:1–6 to destroy these peoples before entering and settling the land of Canaan (compare Deuteronomy 20:17–18). In the Torah, descendants of the Ammonites, Moabites and Egyptians were not permitted to enter the assembly of Israel for some generations (Deuteronomy 23:1–8), but now it seems they should not be admitted to Israel at all.

All these peoples had their own gods and religious practices. But Israel was meant to be a holy nation, separate and chosen to worship God alone; a beacon of light, showing all nations how to live according to God's holy law, and through whom all nations would be blessed (Genesis 12:1–3). Exodus 34:10–16 warns against intermarriage because of the risk of worshipping those other gods and participating in practices that were not acceptable to God – idolatry, sexual immorality, divination, sacrificing children and so on. These are the kinds of 'abominations' of which Ezra speaks.

When Ezra studies the law, he looks back and sees the failures of kings, prophets and priests to live up to this separate, chosen identity and to worship God exclusively. Where the leaders failed, the people followed, and the result was exile. This is why Ezra is so appalled. The returned exiles, who have borne the punishment for past failings, are the 'remnant', the 'holy seed' (Isaiah 6:13) who were meant to become true Israel again, separate and holy to God. And yet they have already begun making the same mistakes as their ancestors.

Ezra's first response is to fast and pray, explicitly connecting the current situation with the ancient prohibition. He acknowledges their guilt and the threat this could pose to the survival of the remnant. His prayer is accompanied by outward signs of mourning and grief – torn clothes, kneeling, weeping, with hands stretched out toward God. Whatever the problem, prayer and confession are a good place to begin.

5 What to do about the foreign women

Ezra 10:1–17

Ezra's demonstrative prayer and confession draw a crowd, and the people join in weeping with him. Then Shecaniah proposes a solution to the problem of intermarriage. He suggests the returned exiles 'make a covenant with our God to send away all these wives and their children' and that this be done 'according to the law' (v. 3). Shecaniah urges Ezra to act, and Ezra does, first ensuring the priests, the Levites and 'all Israel' are all in agreement and making them swear to support him.

In due course, the returned exiles meet together and Ezra gives the instruction: 'Make confession to the Lord the God of your ancestors and do his will; separate yourselves from the peoples of the land and from the foreign wives' (v. 11). The assembly agree with the proposal, but ask for more time – perfectly reasonable, given the rainy conditions. Once again, Ezra gathers a team, and it becomes the task of these officials to 'examine the matter', working out who will be affected by the instruction (v. 16). Finally, they 'come to the end of all the men who had married foreign women' (v. 17). It seems all that remains is for the plan to be executed.

It is worth noting, however, that while Shecaniah advocates sending the foreign wives away 'according to the law', the law does not actually address the exact situation facing the returned exiles. It prohibits intermarriage with other peoples, but it does not prescribe what to do if a marriage has already taken place. Ezra and the returned exiles are therefore required to innovate, based on their understanding and interpretation of the law, and the unprecedented situation they find themselves in. How often do we find ourselves in a similar situation, searching the scriptures for an 'answer' to a problem that is nowhere explicitly addressed? Their innovation highlights the value of studying scripture within interpretive communities, together applying their understanding of ancient words to novel situations and seeking to discern the 'apt word' for the time. It also highlights the difficulty in doing so. Not all the assembly are of the same mind, with four men named in opposition to the plan (v. 15). As the book ends, there will be some ambiguity as to whether the expulsion of women and children ever actually happened.

6 'They sent them away with their children'?

Ezra 10:18–44

The book of Ezra closes with another genealogical record – a record of all 'who had married foreign women', beginning with the priests, then the Levites, then the rest of Israel. The final verse reads: 'All these had married foreign women, and they sent them away with their children' (compare 1 Esdras 9:36). The meaning of the Hebrew is uncertain, however, and an alternative translation reads: 'All these had married foreign women, and some of them had children by these wives' (NIV).

There is therefore some uncertainty as to whether the returned exiles followed through with the plan to send the women and children away. Certainly, Ezra made them swear to do it; certainly, the people agreed (apart from the four dissenters). But the book ends with ambiguity, and, when we look back upon Ezra, there are other hints that this might not have been the ideal solution.

First, nowhere does God *command* it. The proposal comes from within the community and is based on an interpretation of the law – a valid interpretation, perhaps, but also a particularly strict one. This is a community attempting to be faithful to the law and avoid the mistakes of the past. When new challenges arise, there is a need to work out how to apply the law to new situations, because there is no precedent for what to do upon return from exile to ensure God's continuing favour. In the attempt to 'get it right', Ezra takes a particularly hardline approach to defining the boundaries of the people of God.

Second, nowhere does God *endorse* it. When Ezra is introduced in chapter 7, the text is peppered with references to God's 'gracious hand' being upon him, demonstrating God's favour and ensuring his success. But once the issue of intermarriage is raised in chapter 9, the 'hand of God' is no longer present in the text, and we do not hear directly what God has to say about this situation.

Third, there is some dissent within the community (10:15). Other books of the Bible also take different views on 'foreigners' (e.g. Ruth). Ezra's 'exclusivist approach' is therefore 'not the last word... on the challenge to Israel of living among and with other peoples' (Davis, p. 405). Ezra established the Torah as the normative standard for Israel, but interpretations of Torah varied, and other perspectives existed in the postexilic period (e.g. Isaiah 56:3–7, see further Hayes, pp. 372–73).

Guidelines

In Ezra 7—8, Ezra is sent to reestablish the law in Judah and Jerusalem. The house of God is still important, but the word of God is now to the fore. Ezra is instructed to ensure the people are judged 'according to the laws of your God' and to teach those who don't know them (7:25). In Ezra 9—10, the returned exiles' newfound knowledge of the law makes them realise that intermarriage with the 'peoples of the land' is one factor that led to exile. They then need to work out how to apply the law to their current situation – that some of them have intermarried with the 'peoples of the land'.

- To what extent are the people of God still a people of the book?
- What emphasis is given to knowing, interpreting and teaching scripture in your local context?

Ezra begins his journey to Jerusalem with the gracious hand of God upon him, ensuring he finds favour with Artaxerxes and the return is successful. As the people wrestle with the question of what to do about the foreign wives, however, the hand of God is no longer mentioned.

- Where can you see the hand of God at work in your life? (Sometimes this is easier to recognise in hindsight.)
- Were Ezra and his advisors right to propose sending away the foreign wives and their children? Why, or why not?
- How do you approach situations that the Bible does not directly address?

In Ezra, 'true Israel' is increasingly defined as the community of the 'returned exiles'.

- What are the defining features of the people of God in our time? Where are the boundaries, and how are they determined?

FURTHER READING

Ellen F. Davis, *Opening Israel's Scriptures* (Oxford, 2019), pp. 397–406.
John Goldingay, *Ezra, Nehemiah, and Esther for Everyone* (London, 2012).
Hannah K. Harrington, *The Books of Ezra and Nehemiah* (Grand Rapids, 2022).
Christine Hayes, *Introduction to the Bible* (Yale, 2012), pp. 360–74.
Hindy Najman, 'Ezra,' notes in *The Jewish Study Bible* (Oxford, 2014), pp. 1661–80.

Job 1—13: A geography of suffering

Tanya Marlow

At the age of 31, the best and worst event in my life happened to me: I gave birth. My son is the most wonderful gift God has ever given me, but the labour left me with significant disability, exacerbating a pre-existent illness. For the last 15 years, I have been mostly confined to my bed. My heart-cry to God was, 'If you love me, why are you doing this to me?'

All pastors must be prepared to be asked this impossible question by someone who suffers. I would argue that there is no greater theology on this topic than the book of Job. It is a masterclass on pastoral responses to chronic, unresolved suffering.

Yet Job is often left aside by preachers in favour of the Psalms, and those who do preach it tend to focus on the beginning and the end but don't quite know what to do with the 30 chapters of raw lament, anger and bad theology in the middle. Indeed, it is better to think of the book of Job as a geography of suffering than a theology of suffering, tracing the contours of Job's inner spiritual torment. The reader is told in the beginning and end that Job is righteous, but his lament sounds arrogant and aggressive. Conversely, God's final speech proclaims that Job's friends are wrong, but they sound like they're promoting classic Christian teaching. This makes it a profoundly unsettling book for preachers, but a balm for Christians undergoing a dark night of the soul.

To give enough space to the messy middle, this series will cover the prose prologue and first cycle of Job's dialogue with his friends, leaving the later chapters of Job to be covered in the next edition.

Unless otherwise stated, Bible quotations are taken from the NRSV.

1 Once upon a time

Job 1

It is utterly baffling that Noah's ark is told as a cute, illustrated children's story. This necessarily omits crucial details, like the sacrificing of 'clean' animals when Noah lands, and the rest of humanity drowning without pity. The same story, told dispassionately for adults in Genesis, carries a darker message.

Similarly, within Job, there are various genres, reflecting different interpretations of Job's suffering. From the very first line, 'There was once a man in the land of Uz' (v. 1), the prose prologue (Job 1—2) and epilogue (Job 42:7–17) read like fairytales, and their concept of justice reflects that neatness. The majority of Job (except for Job 28, a standalone poem about wisdom) is a succession of poetic dramatic monologues. The theology there is considerably messier.

Theologian Carol Newsom has described the book of Job as a 'polyphonic text', because there are many 'voices' within it competing for the correct interpretation of Job's tragedy. It is a complex symphony with warring melodies which Newsom describes as a 'contest of moral imaginations'.

The book begins with the moralising fairytale. Job is special: 'blameless and upright' (v. 1). He is also wealthy (vv. 2–3). This association between godliness and prosperity echoes Abraham's journey, who feared God and became wealthy, and other biblical wisdom literature: 'the upright will be blessed. Wealth and riches are in their houses' (Psalm 112:2–3).

It is 'the Designated Accuser' (Job 1:6, MSG), God's prosecutor, who challenges God's pride in Job. Is Job wealthy because he's righteous, or is he righteous because he's wealthy? His worldview is simple and cynical: no human loves God unconditionally; therefore, Job will curse God if he loses 'all that he has' (v. 12). Whenever you're tempted to nihilistic cynicism about human nature in general or rich Christians in particular, remember from whom this viewpoint comes.

The narrator's perspective is reassuring. Job loses his possessions but stoically worships God anyway. It's tempting to preach this clean, happy ending as the only right response to suffering. We sing along with Job, 'Blessed be the name of the Lord' (v. 21). Even here, however, questions lurk. Losing wealth is one thing, but even accounting for ancient Near Eastern attitudes to offspring, losing your children is tragic. Is it fair for God to allow this just to win a bet?

2 Job's wife: callous or compassionate?

Job 2:1–10

The Wicked Witch of the West is the villain of *The Wizard of Oz*. However, the more recent musical, *Wicked*, invites a different interpretation of her character by explaining her backstory. The same person can be understood as villain or victim. Described as 'the devil's helper' by Augustine and the 'organ of Satan' by Calvin, is Job's wife really that bad?

In verses 1–6, the Accuser argues that Job's steadfastness is motivated by self-centredness. Job would gladly sacrifice his wealth and children in exchange for his life, the Accuser argues. The stakes are then significantly raised: this time God afflicts Job's body, too, with 'loathsome sores' (v. 7) and other symptoms including pain (detailed later). As skin diseases were understood as punishment from God (for example, the plagues of Egypt or Miriam's leprosy), everyone interpreted Job's suffering as God's judgement.

Job's anonymous wife gets only two lines: 'Do you still persist in your integrity?', apparently denouncing Job's faithfulness as futile, and 'Curse God, and die' (v. 9), echoing the Accuser's prediction of Job's response. Job therefore rebukes her as foolish and against God, while the narrator praises Job for his sinless, silent acceptance of suffering (v. 10).

But have we, and Job himself, underestimated her? An inter-testamental Jewish folktale reimagines her story more sympathetically, where she wanders the streets, homeless from poverty, longing for rest from her 'toils and pains' (from the *Testament of Job*). She has equally lost her fortune, children and security. Feminist theologian Pardes applauds her bold questioning as a necessary challenge to Job's submissiveness, thereby becoming the catalyst, and perhaps the model, for all Job's subsequent questioning of God.

Alternatively, Job's wife's words may be interpreted differently. Grieving and vulnerable, her motivation may be compassion, not disgust. The word she and the Accuser use is *bārak*. Although it can be euphemistically interpreted as 'curse' (the most likely translation for verse 5), it literally means the opposite: 'bless'. Anticipating his imminent, inevitable death, she therefore pleads for Job to praise God in his last words, remaining faithful to the end: 'Bless God, and die.' Her question can similarly be understood as concern for Job to continue to 'persist in integrity' and not lose faith, echoing God's boast of Job (vv. 3, 9). If so, she speaks for countless other believers, heartbroken by the suffering of terminally ill loved ones, who pray for their death as merciful release. Too often, perhaps, we label victims as villains.

3 Two types of silence

Job 2:11–13

Silences are powerful. Once, I was waiting for a scan of a suspicious lump, which I was 90% sure wasn't cancer. I explained to my friend that I wasn't worried. She looked back at me with love in her eyes and waited. In that supportive space, her silence allowed my hidden anxiety to come to the surface, and I cried unexpected tears.

However, silence isn't always kind. Elise (name changed) announced that she had terminal cancer with less than a year to live. Though some friends kept close to her throughout, many others wrote to her emotionally about what a great friend she was, then kept their distance for the rest of her days. It was as though they had delivered their eulogy prematurely and treated her like she was already dead.

In Job 2, Job's three friends went to him when they heard of his troubles, but 'no one spoke a word to him, for they saw that his suffering was very great' (v. 13). Most preachers use this verse as a positive example of how to pastorally respond to someone's suffering. This is seen as the only thing the comforters did right, before ruining it by speaking condemnation.

However, their silence is actually more like Elise's friends. They go with the best of intentions to 'console and comfort him' (v. 11), but the severity of his sickness shocks them. His symptoms include sores infected with worms (7:5), darkening and shrivelling of the skin (30:30), bad breath (19:17) and emaciation (19:20). No wonder they don't recognise him: he is as good as dead.

So, they have a funeral while he's still alive. They grieve for seven days, a customary mourning period for someone dear to you, like Jacob when his father died (Genesis 50:50; also 1 Samuel 31:13). They also throw dust over their heads, which Old Testament scholars Gordis and Clines identify specifically as a funereal ritual (e.g. 2 Samuel 1:2; Ezekiel 27:30–32).

Too often, we distance ourselves emotionally from others' pain. The Accuser responded to Job's undeserved suffering with cold cynicism. Because witnessing Job's physical decline was unbearable, Job's wife desired Job's death. The friends assumed Job's death and pre-emptively mourned him. When have you ever drifted towards these reactions?

4 I want to die

Job 3

The day that I came home from hospital after giving birth, I felt joyful and relieved. Even though I couldn't walk more than a few steps, I was ready to say along with Job, 'Blessed be the name of the Lord' (1:21). But this wasn't the end of the story. For many people who've survived trauma, their initial emotions can be denial or sheer relief, with the depression emerging later. For me, the despair came a few months after the birth, when nothing had improved.

This helps us to understand the unexpected shift in Job's personality between his stoic acceptance in Job 2 and the deep bitterness of Job 3. Remember that Job's great test is to undergo suffering but not curse God. After seven days of shock and silence, the first thing that comes out of Job's mouth is a curse. He will not curse God, but instead he 'cursed the day of his birth' (v. 1), his very existence. He will not kill himself, but longs 'for death' (v. 1): 'Why did I not die at birth… why was I not buried like a stillborn child?' (vv. 11, 16).

Job wishes to undo his existence, in a reversal of God's creation process. The 'let there be light' of Genesis 1:3 becomes 'let that day be darkness' (v. 4); the stars of Genesis 1:16 are put out (v. 9), and we return to the deep of pre-creation, and the chaos of Leviathan (v. 8).

Listen carefully, though, and we see his true motivation: 'Now I would be lying down and quiet; I would be asleep; then I would be at rest' (v. 13), 'there the weary are at rest' (v. 17).

Job's story doesn't end with the neat theology of the prose narrative, but that is sometimes all that theologians offer to those who are suffering: we must praise God, no matter what happens. Christian leaders need to realise that the same person who copes serenely with great loss may yet fall apart later on, and that is a normal reaction to trauma, even (or especially) for faithful, mature believers. This passage also helps us to remember that what may outwardly appear to be a desire to die is more accurately a longing for rest and relief. Dare we cling to Jesus' promise at such moments, 'I will give you rest' (Matthew 11:28)?

5 God's discipline?

Job 4:1–7, 17–19; 5:8–20

How should we counsel someone who is going through hard times? The letter to the Hebrews seems to hold the answer: 'Endure trials for the sake of discipline. God is treating you as children' (Hebrews 12:7). Even the worst suffering can teach us lessons and therefore be 'for our good' (Hebrews 12:10). When I first became ill, I took this seriously. Maybe God was teaching me to rest more. I would listen to this lesson. I would learn. Still, my 'trials' remained.

Eliphaz, the first of Job's friends to speak, does nothing worse than expound that thoroughly biblical doctrine, and he does so with great sensitivity and care. First, he starts with affirmation of Job's ministry. Job previously 'instructed many' and his words had 'strengthened' others 'who were stumbling' (4:3–4). Then he affirms Job's character: 'Is not your fear of God your confidence, and the integrity of your ways your hope?' (4:6).

Initially, the friends assumed that Job would die, but he is still alive. There is hope! Eliphaz reasons that no one 'innocent ever perished' (4:7). Therefore, God will surely restore him. He appeals to the merciful character of God who helps the vulnerable: 'He sets on high those who are lowly, and those who mourn are lifted to safety' (5:11); 'he saves the needy from the sword of their mouth' (5:15). God will not abandon him to death, because God's purpose is restoration: 'For he wounds, but he binds up; he strikes, but his hands heal' (5:18).

Clearly, Job had done something to offend God, but don't we all make mistakes? There was no shame in that. Eliphaz himself had a revelation that no mortal can be fully righteous compared to God (4:17), and we are flawed people who 'live in houses of clay' (4:19). All Job has to do is 'seek God' (5:8) and 'not despise the discipline of the Almighty' (5:17).

Eliphaz offers Job gentle words of hope. It is a beautiful, pastoral message that is fully biblically justified. There is just one problem: Job was not being disciplined by God; there was no lesson to learn. Similarly, when Jesus died on the cross, that was not a lesson for his own good. Not all suffering is God's discipline.

6 I can't survive this alone

Job 6:1–21

How should Christians pastor traumatised people? The UK Trauma Council defines trauma as someone experiencing events 'so extreme or intense that they overwhelm a person's ability to cope'. Having reacted calmly at first, at this point Job can no longer cope. Job's trauma explains why he responds to Eliphaz's gentle sermonising with unexpected fire and anger, accusing his friends even at this early stage of being 'treacherous' (v. 15).

Eliphaz's speech had minimised Job's suffering, as though it were any other light discipline from the Lord, so Job tries to explain how bad it is. He reaches for metaphors. My suffering is so heavy, so weighty, he explains, that if you put it on one side of the scales you would have to pour all the sand in the world into the opposite scale just to make it balance (vv. 1–3). Job's shouts of desperation are justified, 'Does the wild ass bray over its grass, or the ox low over its fodder?' (v. 5) Just as animals do not whine if they are well-fed, Job has cause for his complaint. Eliphaz's comfort is like 'tasteless food' from which he recoils (vv. 6–7).

If the suffering is too much, then the support is also too little. Job compares his friends to the Palestinian wadis overflowing in the rainy season but in the summertime, just when you really need them, they are nowhere to be found (vv. 15–21). Job is like a traveller from Sheba hoping for water in the desert only to perish (v18–19). Job is 'disappointed' and 'confounded' (v. 20) when his friends 'withhold kindness' (v. 14).

Eliphaz's suggestion of waiting indefinitely for God's restoration is impossible because Job knows he has nothing left in him to get through this. His only hope is in God ending his life (vv. 8–10). With poignant vulnerability he begs for help from his friends, because he is not made of impervious bronze (vv. 11–12), 'In truth I have no help in me, and any resource is driven from me' (v. 13). Job knows he cannot endure this alone.

When we get to the end of ourselves, when we are traumatised or completely overwhelmed, irritable and desperate, we don't need sermons. We need kindness. We need comforters unafraid to look honestly at our calamity (v. 21). We don't need theology; we need friends.

Guidelines

The main purpose of the prose prologue is to set up the scenario of the suffering of a righteous man who is not being punished for his sin but doesn't know it. It is very much framed as a fairytale.

- Why do you think the writer of Job employed this genre for the beginning, which is so different from the dramatic poetry of the remainder of the book?
- What effect does it have on us as a reader and interpreter of Job?
- When a modern reader encounters Job for the first time, often their first reaction is that God is unfair to cause Job so much irreversible suffering, particularly his children's deaths. How might you respond to that?

In my reading of Job, I went against the traditional interpretation of Job's wife and friends' reaction in the prose prologue.

- How do you interpret their initial reactions, and why?
- In what times during your life have you wished for silence and received unwelcome talking instead? And when have you wished for words and received only silence?
- As a pastor, friend or carer, what action do you take when you notice you are beginning to numb yourself to others' pain?

The church rarely talks about suicidal ideation in the context of suffering, yet this is one of the first things that Job articulates. Job openly talks about his desperation, without shame, both to his friends and to God. There are no simple answers, and the church needs to be careful about attempting what psychologists and counsellors are better equipped to treat. However, it is worth thinking through how the church might be a safer place to admit suicidal thoughts. For the sufferer, too, there is an implicit challenge to bring those thoughts in the open before God and trusted others, safe in the knowledge that feeling suicidal is common for righteous people who suffer.

1 Patron saint of chronic illness

Job 7

Once, I had sudden back pain so severe that all I could do was lie still for three hours to stop the spasming and wait to be rescued by my husband. Painkillers barely touched it. First, I cried. Then, I tried everything: breathing deeply, telling myself I was floating above my pain, relaxing my muscles, then reciting *Les Misérables* in my head as a distraction. Time crawled by. The pain would break through again, and I would panic, then cry, then feel angry, then afraid again, then return to my slow breathing. It was three hours; it was an eternity.

The book of Job holds no clear reference to the passage of time, but Job's comment that he has been 'allotted months of emptiness' supports the idea that his condition is chronic, ongoing (v. 3). His illness is relentless, 'my skin hardens, then breaks out again' (v. 5), and his physical pain unbearable, 'so that I would choose strangling and death rather than this body' (v. 15). Neither is there relief with sleep, because God terrifies him with insomnia and nightmares (vv. 4, 14).

For the first time, Job directs his anger at the source of his disease: God. Un-submissive, un-stoic, he vows, 'I will not restrain my mouth… I will complain in the bitterness of my soul' (v. 11). The psalmist's awe-filled marvelling, 'What are human beings that you are mindful of them, mortals that you care for them?' (Psalm 8:4), is subverted into a horror film where there is no escape from God's watchful eye: 'What are human beings that you… test them every moment?' (Job 7:17–18). Job demands to know why he has become God's 'target' (v. 20) and why God refuses to pardon him, if indeed he has sinned (v. 21). God as 'watcher of humanity' (v. 20) is no protective guardian but an oppressive prison guard.

Neither society nor the church know what to do with people in ongoing physical pain or psychological agony. Greek philosophy has a lot to answer for, with the supposed separation of body and soul, and self-help books still proclaim mind over matter. Job admits no such separation. 'I loathe my life,' he summarises (v. 16).

While Christians sympathise with acute medical crises, most seem to expect chronically ill people to be serene saints in constant prayer. If this is so, our patron saint is Job, our virtue is honest anguish, and Job 7 is our prayer.

2 God's justice?

Job 8:1–22

If someone asked you to summarise the character of God in one word, what would it be? For Bildad, God's defining characteristic is justice (v. 3). The image of God as just judge runs throughout the Hebrew Bible and New Testament, and Job himself later expresses his desire to be heard before God as his judge. The problem with Bildad's speech isn't his theology; it's his application.

For Bildad, God's justice means there is no such thing as tragedy; all misfortune must be divine retribution. This leads him to proclaim that Job's children deserved their fate, pressing his thumb into Job's wound. Job's great fear was his children '[sinning] and [cursing] God in their hearts', so he made pre-emptory sacrifices on their behalf (Job 1:5). Bildad now twists Job's action into evidence that his children's sin deserved early death, 'It's plain that your children sinned against him – otherwise, why would God have punished them?' (Job 8:4, MSG).

Whereas Eliphaz found wisdom through mystical revelation and traditional teaching, Bildad looks to proverbs from ancient ancestors. In comparison to wisdom of the primordial forefathers, he and Job 'know nothing' (vv. 8–10). Bildad offers a wisdom parable, similar to Psalm 1 and Jeremiah 17:5–8, where a withering plant symbolises 'all who forget God' (vv. 12–13) and the righteous are like a well-watered plant, secure and firm. I prefer Habel's translation of verse 16, 'Another plant stays fresh, even in the sun' (*The Book of Job*, 1985), describing the longevity of the 'blameless' (v. 20). His appeal to Job is thus the same as Eliphaz's: 'Seek God and make supplication to the Almighty' (v. 5), because God restores the fortunes of the 'pure and upright' (v. 6).

The speech is thick with irony. Bildad's patronising assertion that Job knows nothing is actually truer of himself. Bildad believes the children were punished for wickedness, but they were simply caught in the crosshairs of Job's test. He hints that Job is forgetting God (v. 13) but, as we've seen in Job 7, Job is constantly aware of God. He is eerily right that God will restore Job's fortunes (vv. 6–7, 21–22), but wrong that this is contingent on repentance.

Bildad's sermon is dangerous because it is right in principle and wrong in practice. It serves as a warning to all preachers: beware assigning God's judgement to the world's tragedies. God's justice is bigger, more complex, than mere cause and effect.

3 There's nothing that he cannot do

Job 9:1–24, 32–35

As a child, I sang, 'My God is so big, so strong and so mighty.' The song goes on to list examples of God's reassuring omnipotence through creation: mountains, rivers and stars.

For Job, however, God's almighty power has a darker side: 'there's nothing that he cannot do' includes destroying as well as creating. God 'removes mountains' in anger (v. 5); God, who made the rivers, 'trampled the waves of the Sea' (v. 8) and destroyed Rahab (v. 13), an ancient mythological sea monster signifying chaos and evil. The God who made 'Bear and Orion' (v. 9) also 'seals up the stars' and can take away the sun (v. 7).

Eliphaz claims that only '[the wicked] perish' (Job 4:9) and Bildad says that proves Job's children were wicked (Job 8:4). However, Job knows one thing the friends don't: he really is blameless. There must be another explanation. Job points to natural disasters, corrupt judges and evil yet successful landowners (vv. 23–24) and concludes, 'God destroys both the blameless and the wicked' (v. 22). Job is not necessarily attacking the character of God. Rather, this is the logical conclusion of God's right to give and take away, as Job initially stated (Job 1:21; 2:10). After all, Jesus expressed a similar sentiment: God 'sends rain on the righteous and on the unrighteous' (Matthew 5:45).

Even so, Job's own answer doesn't quite satisfy him, because he longs to be declared right before God. He takes Eliphaz's rhetorical question, 'Can mortals be righteous before God?' (Job 4:17) and reinterprets it as a genuine proposal, 'How can a mortal be [declared righteous] before God?' (Job 9:2). Job's tentative solution is to present his case at a divine court, complaining that God 'multiplies my wounds without cause' (v. 17). But if God is so terrifying as to afflict Job without reason, how could Job trust that God would allow a fair trial without destroying him? Alas, there is no mediator or adjudicator between them (vv. 32–33).

Even though Job's healthy fear of God has transformed into terror, he still longs for reconciliation. Job's suffering has not quite extinguished his spiritual desire. We must remember: anyone who asks abstract theological questions about why God destroys the unrighteous and righteous alike is almost always carrying a deeply personal issue, usually involving ongoing suffering, confusion and a desire for a go-between to reunite them with God.

4 I do not know myself

Job 9:21; 10:1–17

For many people, the miracle of becoming a parent brings them closer to God. For me, parenthood almost made me abandon God. I delighted in my baby daily and was shocked by the strength of my love for this tiny stranger. As the months went on, however, my disability and pain worsened, and my suffering increased. Eventually, I snapped. 'Supposedly, I am your dearly loved child,' I railed at God. 'But I know now that I would do anything in my power to stop my child suffering. Why are you letting me suffer like this?'

Job had similar trouble understanding God's actions. He turns from theology to honest prayer, a bitter complaint against God (vv. 1–3). Job's lament uses similar language to Psalm 139, describing the loving care God took to create him, 'Your hands fashioned me and made me… you fashioned me like clay… you clothed me with skin and flesh and knit me together with bones and sinews' (vv. 8–11). Job has walked alongside God for most of his life and can testify to God's former goodness to him: 'You have granted me life and steadfast love, and your care has preserved my spirit' (v. 12).

Yet now, God is attacking him and seemingly undoing all that effort and care: 'Will you turn me to dust again?… curdle me like cheese?' (vv. 9–10). Job appeals to God's logic: 'Does it seem good to you to oppress, to despise the work of your hands?' (v. 3). It makes no sense. With his friends, Job is confident in his argumentation, but before God, we see his insecurity and confusion emerge. He's convinced that he's blameless. But perhaps he's actually sinful? If so, God could forgive him, yet he's still being punished (v. 14). If he were wicked, he would deserve punishment, but if he's righteous and suffering unfairly, then he still loses, because God is attacking him (vv. 14–17).

Job's internal turmoil and confusion is poignantly distilled in his blurted-out exclamation, 'I am blameless! I do not know myself! I loathe my life!' (Job 9:21, exclamation marks added). My own suffering prompted similar thoughts, 'I don't deserve this! (Do I secretly deserve this?) Surely God created me and my son. Why is God allowing this? Am I bad, or is God?' When suffering comes, it can both shake our view of God and shatter our sense of ourselves. We are more fragile than we might appear.

5 God's mysterious ways?

Job 11

The famous preacher stood on the stage. I was there at the front, sitting in the special wheelchair section. 'Instinctively, we feel like suffering is unfair,' he began. He looked at the disabled section directly. 'Your suffering isn't unfair; it's your blessings that are unfair. We have all sinned and deserve the full extent of God's wrath. God treats us all better than we deserve.'

I wonder if he knew that he was quoting Zophar, Job's non-comforting comforter, almost word for word: 'Know then that God exacts of you less than your guilt deserves' (v. 6). Zophar, supposedly Job's friend, looked upon his festering skin and emaciated flesh, the extreme levels of suffering and grief he was enduring, and decided that Job's suffering ought to be more severe.

Whereas Eliphaz drew his authority from supernatural visions and Bildad appealed to ancient proverbs of the forefathers, Zophar points to God's hidden, esoteric wisdom, 'But oh, that God would speak… and that he would tell you the secrets of wisdom!… It is higher than heaven… Deeper than Sheol – what can you know?' (vv. 5–8). With no trace of irony, Zophar suggests that although Job cannot fathom the 'deep things of God' (v. 7), Zophar himself has a pretty good grip on them. Zophar declares Job 'worthless', iniquitous, and a babbler of vain talk (vv. 2–3, 11–12), which makes him a fool (Proverbs 10:8–19). Just as a wild donkey will never give birth to a human, so a fool will never get wisdom (v. 12); Job is a lost cause.

Nevertheless, Zophar promises restoration if only Job repents (vv. 13–20), which has been the unifying theme of the friends' speeches in this first cycle. If only Job would be silent, confess he deserves his suffering and repent, then he will be restored. When God finally speaks, however, it is Zophar's callous words that are condemned, not Job's honest lament.

Anyone can be insensitive to a person in pain, but in my experience it is only Christians who are cruel enough to pronounce 'you deserve worse' over a child with bone cancer, in the name of theology. It is all too easy to caricature Job's friends, but any disabled person can tell you that Job's comforters are still living, breathing and speaking condemnation to suffering people today.

6 I will not be silent

Job 13:1–26

The book of Job is not so much a theology of suffering as it is a geography of suffering. The prologue set up Job's test: if a God-fearing person loses everything and suffers physically, will they curse God and turn their back on their faith? Throughout this first cycle of speeches, we watch with bated breath to see whether Job will indeed curse God or accept suffering stoically. He does neither. He curses his life, his birth, his body, but he does not curse God. Rather, he questions God; he rails at God; he raises his complaint.

His friends cannot understand why Job doesn't simply confess his sin, offer sacrifices and repentant prayer, so he will be restored. But Job is too truthful for that. He doesn't know why God is doing this, but he does know he is 'blameless'. This doesn't necessarily mean 'completely without sin', as in the apostle Paul's theology. After all, Job has invited God to reveal any remnant of sin in him (v. 23), made offerings in the past for any potential sin, and even frets about forgotten 'iniquities of my youth' (v. 26). However, both God and Job agree that there is no unaddressed sin in Job's life. Job emphatically does not deserve his suffering.

Though the friends offered no comfort, 'worthless physicians' that they were (v. 4), their bad theology ironically roused Job's soul and prodded him to wrestle with God. In his first speech, Job, exhausted and defeated, begged for imminent death. By Job 13, we see a fresh energy and determination. His primary desire has switched from ending his suffering to being declared righteous by God.

The one thing Job refuses to do is suffer in submissive silence, even if it costs him his life: 'I will speak, and let come on me what may... I will defend my ways to his face' (vv. 13–15). Job wants his day in court with God (v. 18). His only requests are protection from further terror, and a response from God (vv. 20–22). In the end, he receives both, though not in that order.

Ultimately, Job, with all his raging rants, is judged to have spoken rightly of God, in contrast to the friends (42:7). If today you are suffering, angry and confused, fling it all at God. Job did.

Guidelines

I have called Job the 'patron saint of chronic illness'. Most commentators miss the fact that the majority of Job's complaints are focused on his diseased body, yet in church it is rare that ongoing physical suffering is addressed as a pastoral issue. Typically, society and the church are understanding of struggle in the initial stages of an illness, but not ongoing complaint. Yet Job keeps returning to his physical suffering and bemoaning it, much to the frustration of his friends.

If you are a church leader:

- How might you allow more space for prayers of lament?
- What is your instinctive reaction to someone who keeps complaining about the same thing?
- How might the church become a safer space for people dealing with trauma or chronic suffering?
- How might Job's experience influence how you preach on suffering as God's discipline, God's justice or God's wisdom?

If you are a chronic sufferer:

- Is your response to God more like Job's initial reaction in the prose prologue, or his extended complaint?
- What are the merits of both?
- What comfort have you found so far in Job's words?
- What scares you, if anything, about Job's approach?

FURTHER READING

Francis I. Anderson, *Job* (IVP, 1976).
Richard P. Belcher Jr, *Finding Favour in the Sight of God* (IVP, 2018).
David J. A . Clines, *Job 1–20 (Word Biblical Commentary Vol. 17)* (Zondervan, 1989).
Norman C. Habel, *The Book of Job* (SCM Press, 1985).
Norman C. Habel, *God Trauma and Wisdom Therapy* (Fortress Press, 2024).
John E. Hartley, *The Book of Job* (William B Eerdmans, 1988).
Carol A. Newsom, *The Book of Job* (OUP, 2003).

SHARING OUR VISION – MAKING A GIFT

I would like to make a donation to support BRF Ministries.
Please use my gift for:

☐ Where it is most needed ☐ Anna Chaplaincy ☐ BRF Resources
☐ Messy Church ☐ Parenting for Faith

Title	First name/initials	Surname

Address

	Postcode

Email

Telephone

Signature	Date

Please accept my gift of:

☐ £2 ☐ £5 ☐ £10 ☐ £20 Other £ ______

by (*delete as appropriate*):

☐ Cheque/Charity Voucher payable to 'BRF'

☐ MasterCard/Visa/Debit card/Charity card

Name on card

Card no. ☐☐☐☐ ☐☐☐☐ ☐☐☐☐ ☐☐☐☐

Expires end M M Y Y

Signature	Date

Please complete other side of form ➔

BRF Ministries Gift Aid Declaration

In order to Gift Aid your donation, you must tick the box below.

☐ I want to Gift Aid my donation and any donation I make in the future or have made in the past four years to BRF Ministries

I am a UK taxpayer and understand that if I pay less Income Tax and/or Capital Gains Tax in the current tax year than the amount of Gift Aid claimed on all my donations, it is my responsibility to pay any difference.

Please notify BRF Ministries if you want to cancel this Gift Aid declaration, change your name or home address, or no longer pay sufficient tax on your income and/or capital gains.

You can also give online at **brf.org.uk/donate**, which reduces our administration costs, making your donation go further.

Our ministry is only possible because of the generous support of individuals, churches, trusts and gifts in wills.

☐ I would like to leave a gift to BRF Ministries in my will.
Please send me further information.

☐ I would like to find out about giving a regular gift to BRF Ministries.

For help or advice regarding making a gift, please contact our fundraising team +44 (0)1865 319700

Your privacy

We will use your personal data to process this transaction. From time to time we may send you information about the work of BRF Ministries that we think may be of interest to you. Our privacy policy is available at **brf.org.uk/privacy**. Please contact us if you wish to discuss your mailing preferences.

Registered with FUNDRAISING REGULATOR

Please complete other side of form

Please return this form to 'Freepost BRF'

No other address information or stamp is needed

Bible Reading Fellowship is a charity (233280) and company limited by guarantee (301324), registered in England and Wales

Overleaf... Guidelines forthcoming issue | Author profile | Recommended reading | Order and subscription forms

Guidelines forthcoming issue

The upcoming issue of *Guidelines* is packed with wisdom, insight, celebration, lament and challenge. I hope you will join us to discover the riches it contains!

'The Christian life is a matter of waiting and preparing, coming ever closer to the Lord' – so writes Henry Wansbrough as he encourages us to approach Advent with the right frame of mind. He explores a range of texts from the Old Testament, from the gospels and from Paul's letters through this important season of preparing our hearts.

With the Christmas period often full of rampant consumerism and overspending, Sarah Edwards encourages us to consider ethical finance. Sarah works with the JustMoney movementa and he hopes 'to help make connections between money and our faith, understanding what this means for how we live individually and corporately, and how we speak out prophetically to the world around us'.

We are also offered a range of notes on Old Testament texts: Bill Goodman begins a two-part series looking in depth at Deuteronomy; Miriam Bier Hinksman offers us new insight into the sometimes overly-familiar story of Ruth; Victoria Omotoso brilliantly brings to life the book of Joel and invites us to discover God's enduring presence with us; Amy Scott Robinson looks at Jeremiah's prophetic images and what they teach us about God and his character; and finally Tanya Marlow finishes off her brilliant and challenging series on Job.

In the New Testament, Steve Walton kicks off our study of Mark (Andy Angel and Isabelle Hamley will continue this series in subsequent issues), covering the first eight chapters in detail. Andy Angels takes us through 1 and 2 Thessalonians, drawing out how they give us unique insight into the crises, passions and experiences of our early forebears in faith. Helen Miller explores Revelation, encouraging us to see the primary focus of this book as Jesus.

As ever, may these offering in *Guidelines* expand your vision of God and Christ, and lead you closer to the God who loves you infinitely.

What the Bible means to me: Tim Welch

The Bible still amazes me for its power to speak relevantly into my life, and into the lives of other people, with just the right word at just the right time. I first experienced this mystery as an undergraduate, when a simple gospel story was read and explained via preaching, and I (and countless other students) immediately responded, having clearly heard the call of Jesus. Through this Bible engagement, it was as if Jesus stepped off the page and walked right into my life, changing everything.

Since then, not every encounter with scripture has been as dramatic, yet I have identified a pattern that the Bible really does serve as a 'lamp to my feet and a light to my path' (Psalm 119:105). Usually, it is in the quiet place, where a regular diet of Bible reading teaches, challenges, and helps form my daily discipleship. But at some of my most desperate times in life, as I have struggled with depression and inadequacy, I find the Bible contains rich resources to meet me (and others) in our desperation.

Most recently, when reading Psalm 18, David's song of deliverance became my theme tune for a few weeks, with assurances of God being my rock and fortress, and the vivid image of David being saved from a cave and enabled to stand 'secure on the heights' like a deer captured my imagination with helpful relief, strength and hope (18:33).

The mystery of the Bible's impact has also shaped my Christian ministry. The privilege of serving God in pastoral work and in a theological college often heightened my felt sense of human weakness. Yet Bible engagement in one-to-ones, small groups and preaching is perhaps my best evidence that even when I am woefully weak, the word of God continues to work powerfully and deeply in me and through me.

So probably the passage which best describes my personal experience of Bible reading over 40+ years is Jesus joining the two disciples on Emmaus Road (Luke 24: 13-35). I admit the aptness of Jesus' words, 'How foolish you are and how slow of heart to believe' (v. 25), and my life and ministry experience mirrors the two who walked that road, with hearts that were 'burning within… while he was opening the scriptures' (v. 32).

Hence, I maintain a deep conviction that an opened Bible and attentive posture still have power for the Word and Spirit to change lives. My story from multiple contexts is that 'the word of God is not chained' (2 Timothy 2:9), and thankfully even now in my YMCA chaplaincy role I'm still seeing the Bible's power as Jesus saves and mends broken lives.

Recommended reading

A biblical exposition with testimonies of contemporary migration. In *Come for Refuge*, Pete Wilcox, Bishop of Sheffield, invites you to read the book of Ruth through the lens of the present global migration crisis. By interweaving an exposition of the text of Ruth with testimonies from contemporary migrants, creating a conversation between the two, this book offers a hopeful vision of what migration can contribute to the world. An essential study guide for individuals and churches.

The following is an edited extract taken from the introduction.

The book of Ruth is the story not just of one woman, but of two: Ruth and Naomi. The whole narrative is only four chapters long: Naomi is most prominent in chapters 1 and 4 (though Ruth is present), and Ruth in chapters 2 and 3 (though Naomi is present). Both women had experience of migration: Naomi was an Israelite who went to live as a migrant in the land of Moab; Ruth was a Moabite who went to live as a migrant in the land of Israel. For Naomi, migration was essentially a bitter experience; for Ruth, a much more fulfilling one – she sought and found refuge (the word is used of her in 2:12) in Bethlehem and almost certainly never returned to her country of origin.

This exposition of the book of Ruth seeks to pay particular attention to those experiences of migration. I would argue that the text invites this focus, not least by the way in which it repeatedly places stress on Ruth's migrant status: again and again, sometimes gratuitously, she is described as 'Ruth the Moabite' and once she is described as 'the Moabite… from the country of Moab' (2:6). Once she describes herself as 'a foreigner' (2:10) – in Hebrew, *nākerîyāh*, an alien.

However, my sensitivity to this emphasis in the book of Ruth has been heightened by my recent interactions with migrants and refugees in the two cities in the UK in which I have lived in the past twelve years: specifically with refugees and asylum seekers from Iran, Kurdistan, and Ukraine. Their stories of leaving a beloved homeland, of risk-laden journeys, of uncertain and uneven welcomes in a new and deeply unfamiliar country have enriched (among other things) my reading of this biblical text.

That enrichment is what has prompted me to experiment with the format in this book. I have tried to create a conversation between the experience of Ruth and Naomi, on the one hand, and that of some contemporary migrants, refugees, and asylum seekers, on the other. I am deeply grateful to those individuals who confided their stories in me and who have trusted me to place their testimonies alongside the Bible story. How far this experiment is a success will be for others to judge, but I am immensely grateful to those whose risky frankness with me made the experiment possible. I am especially thankful to those who provided me with testimonies which, on account of various inevitable editorial considerations, I have not ultimately been able to include in this book. Their generosity, patience, grace, and understanding have been exemplary.

These testimonies are drawn from two contexts: Sheffield, England, where I serve as bishop of the Anglican Diocese, and Melbourne, Australia, where I drafted much of this book during a period of sabbatical leave. As the bishop of Sheffield, it is my privilege to be one of the patrons of a magnificent charity called ASSIST, which seeks to support some of the most vulnerable people in our City of Sanctuary. So it was an obvious step, not least as a way of drawing attention to the extraordinary work of the staff and volunteers of ASSIST, to seek to secure some of these testimonies from among those the charity has supported – though not all the 'Sheffield' stories are 'ASSIST' stories.

Part of the point of this book is to underline that migration is a global challenge requiring a global response. Our experience of increased migration to the UK in recent decades is by no means unique – quite the opposite. On sabbatical, I had barely been in Melbourne for 48 hours before I became aware of the extent of migration to that city at present and of the work of the Anglican Church in seeking to support asylum seekers, refugees, and other migrants there. The opportunity to include testimonies from migrants to Melbourne seemed, in the providence of God, too good to miss; and I am delighted that it has proved possible.

The challenge of rising global migration and government policy

Migration has been growing globally for decades. The World Migration Report for 2022, published by the United Nations' International Organisation for Migration (IOM), estimates that 'there were around 281 million international migrants in the world in 2020, which equates to 3:6 per cent of the global population'. It goes on to state that this number is '128 million more than in 1990 and over three times the estimated number in 1970'.

Some definitions will be useful at this point, and I have been working with those offered by the IOM. It uses the word 'migrant' as an umbrella term with the broadest possible scope, to refer to any person who for any reason now lives in a country other than the country of their birth. In this sense students studying overseas, for example, are migrants. According to the 1951 Convention relating to the Status of Refugees, cited by the IOM, the term 'refugee' has a much narrower meaning. It refers to 'persons who, owing to a well-founded fear of persecution for reasons of race, religion, nationality, membership of a particular social group or political opinion, are outside the country of their nationality and are unable or, owing to such fear, are unwilling to avail themselves of the protection of that country'. Thirdly, again using the IOM definition, an asylum seeker is 'someone whose claim has not yet been finally decided on by the country in which he or she has submitted it. Not every asylum seeker will ultimately be recognized as a refugee, but every recognized refugee is initially an asylum seeker'.

Every refugee and asylum seeker is therefore a migrant, but by no means is every migrant a refugee or asylum seeker. Migrants may be relatively prosperous and may exercise substantial freedom of choice and agency in making a migration. Obviously, however, there are also many migrants who are not prosperous and who have little freedom of choice or agency when they migrate; they might best be described as 'forced migrants'. These include increasing numbers of trafficked persons and increasing numbers of climate migrants (seeking to escape famine and drought for example), as well as migrants who are fleeing conflict or war. The testimonies of contemporary migrants in this book are exclusively those of refugees and asylum seekers – of migrants who have found themselves in vulnerable situations. Although 'forced migrants' is not a happy phrase, and not a universally accepted one, I use it to emphasise the vulnerability, not least, of Ruth in the Bible story.

It is interesting to note that the IOM has an essentially positive disposition towards the phenomenon of migration, even towards globally increasing migration, seeing it as part of the solution to the world's great problems, rather than as a contributor to them. In its 'Institutional Strategy on Migration and Sustainable Development', the IOM argues that 'migration, when well managed, can be both a development strategy and a development outcome', contributing to, rather than hindering, the achievement of the UN's sustainable development goals. It notes, for example, that many migrants are economically productive and benefit not only their country of residence but their country of origin too. The IOM estimates that 'remittances' (financial or in-kind transfers made by migrants directly to families or communities in their countries of origin) increased from US$128 billion in 2000 to US$831 billion in 2022. Of course, what migrants contribute to both their country of residence and their country of origin should not be measured purely financially.

This rather positive stance towards global migration is noticeably at odds with recent government policy in the UK. For well over a decade, until July 2024, the Conservative government sought to respond to (indeed, to combat) increasing migration by the creation of a so-called 'hostile environment' – 'a range of measures aimed at identifying and reducing the number of immigrants in the UK with no right to remain', which by 2018 had shockingly led to the wrongful deportation of at least 63 members of the Windrush Generation. Although the terminology was generally abandoned latterly (in favour of 'a compliant environment'), the policy has not. Thus during 2023, the government introduced the Illegal Immigration Act (designed not least to 'stop the boats' crossing the English Channel) and procured the Bibby Stockholm accommodation barge as a holding centre for asylum seekers awaiting the outcome of their claims. A treaty with Rwanda was also signed in December that year, with the associated legislation placed before Parliament in 2024, to enable asylum seekers to be removed there. Only the General Election in July 2024 and the consequential change of government prevented the passage of the Rwanda legislation and the implementation of the treaty. Those measures were all highly controversial: indeed, the earliest attempt to arrange the deportation of asylum seekers in the UK to Rwanda was ruled unlawful by the UK's own Supreme Court in December 2022.

Of course, hard cases make bad law, and the book of Ruth is not a policy document. It goes without saying that it is neither possible nor appropriate to extrapolate from the experience of two individuals in a setting over 2,000 miles from Britain and over 3,000 years ago to contemporary national government policy. However, national government policy becomes inhumane precisely when it loses sight of its impact on individual migrants. So the book of Ruth may nevertheless helpfully encourage us to reflect on what good government policy can look like and what kind of outcomes it might enable.

To assist in such reflection, this book includes study materials, primarily designed for group use but also capable of being used by individuals. There are study materials to accompany each of the six main chapters of the book, each set including questions both about the biblical text and about the experience of contemporary migrants, as well as suggestions for worship and for further activity.

To order a copy of this book, please use the order form or visit ***brfresources.org.uk***.

Coming soon from BRF Resources

Written by two practitioners in this field, *Dementia, God and the Church* aims to show how person-centred approaches to dementia can provide hope. Wendy Gleadle first examines the difficulties of maintaining religious beliefs as cognition declines, and the implications of this if faith is equally emotional as cognitive. Frances Attwood asks how churches can better support those living with dementia, through examining what they and their families and carers find helpful and want most.

Dementia, God and the Church
Journeying with hope
Wendy Gleadle and Frances Attwood
978 1 80039 433 9 £12.99 (coming July 2026)
brfresources.org.uk

Coming soon from BRF Resources

With thoughtful research, pastoral insight, and honest stories, *Treasures in Straw* explores the themes of loss and blessing throughout the nativity. Against a darker backdrop, we see with greater clarity God's unexpected generosity and our unshakeable blessings. However you feel about Christmas, this book will leave you with fresh hope, deeper understanding, and genuine joy in living with Christ.

Treasures in Straw
Exploring the griefs and gifts of the Christmas story
Tanya Marlow
978 0 85746 567 1 £9.99 (coming August 2026)
brfresources.org.uk

In *To Hell's Mouth and Back* Trystan Owain Hughes explores his experience of suffering, considering how God can redeem and transform pain and disability, and examines how common experiences of pilgrimage are echoed in the challenges of our life journeys. Along the way, the reader is led to consider the journeys we all face, as we search for God's presence and hope in our joys and pains.

To Hell's Mouth and Back
Pilgrimage, suffering and hope
Trystan Owain Hughes
978 1 80039 426 1 £9.99
brfresources.org.uk

Belonging without Barriers casts a vision of inclusion and full belonging within our churches and other Christian communities for those with additional needs. Each chapter contains up-to-date research, personal accounts, interviews and a range of specific, actionable ideas, including changes that any individual within the church could make. Throughout, the emphasis is that this is an 'every believer ministry' as we all grow in love together as Christ's disciples wherever he has put us.

Belonging without Barriers
Creating accessible Christian communities
Triona Brading, Lois Bunyan and Claire Wood
978 0 85746 882 6 £14.99
brfresources.org.uk

Growing in Prayer will help individuals and groups develop their prayer life. It can be used by anyone to help you explore new ways of praying at home or in the church community, on your own or in groups. It offers a brief introduction to twelve different ways of praying and gives space for you to practise, develop and reflect on what you have learned.

Growing in Prayer
Exploring 12 different ways to pray for individuals and groups
Edited by Susanne Carlsson
978 1 80039 506 0 £9.99
brfresources.org.uk

Tony Horsfall explores six Bible stories that describe individuals encountering God, showing how we can learn how to notice the presence of the divine for ourselves. He also unpacks key spiritual practices that anyone can follow, and introduces insights from influential writers on the awareness of God in the ordinary.

Attentive to God
Being aware of God's presence in daily life
Tony Horsfall
978 0 85746 401 8 £9.99
brfresources.org.uk

To order

Online: **brfresources.org.uk**
Telephone: **+44 (0)1865 319700**
Mon–Fri 9.30–17.00

Delivery times within the UK are normally 15 working days. Prices are correct at the time of going to press but may change without prior notice.

Title	Price	Qty	Total
Come for Refuge	£9.99		
Dementia, God and the Church	£12.99		
Treasures in Straw	£9.99		
The Cost of Christian Living	£9.99		
To Hell's Mouth and Back	£9.99		
Belonging without Barriers	£14.99		
Growing in Prayer	£9.99		
Attentive to God	£9.99		

POSTAGE AND PACKING CHARGES			
Order value	UK	Europe	Rest of world
Under £7.00	£2.00	Available on request	Available on request
£7.00–£29.99	£3.00		
£30.00 and over	FREE		

Total value of books	
Donation*	
Postage and packing	
Total for this order	

* Please complete and return the Gift Aid declaration on page 138.

Please complete in BLOCK CAPITALS

Title ________ First name/initials ______________ Surname ______________________________

Address ____

____ Postcode ______________

Acc. No. ________________________ Telephone ______________________________

Email ____

Method of payment

❑ Cheque (made payable to BRF) ❑ MasterCard / Visa

Card no. ☐☐☐☐ ☐☐☐☐ ☐☐☐☐ ☐☐☐☐

Expires end ☐☐ ☐☐ (M M Y Y)

We will use your personal data to process this order. From time to time we may send you information about the work of BRF Ministries. Please contact us if you wish to discuss your mailing preferences. **brf.org.uk/privacy**

Registered with FUNDRAISING **REGULATOR**

Please return this form to:

BRF Ministries, 15 The Chambers, Vineyard, Abingdon OX14 3FE | **enquiries@brf.org.uk**

For terms and cancellation information, please visit **brfresources.org.uk/terms**.

BRF Ministries needs you!

If you're one of our regular *Guidelines* readers, you will know all about the benefits and blessings of regular Bible study and the value of serious daily notes to guide, inform and challenge you.

Here are some recent comments from *Guidelines* readers:

> *'... very thoughtful and spiritually helpful. [These notes] are speaking to the church as it is today, and therefore to Christians like us who live in today's world.'*

> *'You have assembled an amazingly diverse group of people and their contributions are most certainly thoughtful.'*

If you have similarly positive things to say about *Guidelines*, would you be willing to share your experience with others? Could you ask for a brief slot during church notices or write a short piece for your church magazine or website? Do you belong to groups, formal or informal, academic or professional, where you could share your experience of using *Guidelines* and encourage others to try them?

It doesn't need to be complicated: just answering these three questions in what you say or write will get your message across:

- How do *Guidelines* Bible study notes help you grow in knowledge and faith?
- Where, when and how do you use them?
- What would you say to people who haven't yet tried them?

We can supply further information if you need it and would love to hear about it if you do give a talk or write an article.

For more information:

- Email **enquiries@brf.org.uk**
- Telephone BRF Ministries on **+44 (0)1865 319700** Mon–Fri 9.30–17.00
- Write to us at BRF Ministries, 15 The Chambers, Vineyard, Abingdon OX14 3FE

Inspiring people of all ages to grow in Christian faith

At BRF Ministries, we long for people of all ages to grow in faith and understanding of the Bible. That's what all our work as a charity is about.

- Our **BRF Resources** help Christians go deeper in their understanding of scripture, in prayer and in their walk with God. Our conferences and events bring people together to share this journey, while our Holy Habits resources help whole congregations grow together as disciples of Jesus, living out and sharing their faith.
- We also want to make it easier for local churches to engage effectively in ministry and mission – by helping them bring new families into a growing relationship with God through **Messy Church** or by supporting churches as they nurture the spiritual life of older people through **Anna Chaplaincy**.
- Our **Parenting for Faith** team coaches parents and others to raise God-connected children and teens, and enables churches to fully support them.

Do you share our vision?

Though a significant proportion of BRF Ministries' funding is generated through our charitable activities, we are dependent on the generous support of individuals, churches and charitable trusts.

If you share our vision, would you help us to enable even more people of all ages to grow in faith? Your prayers and financial support are vital for the work that we do. You could:

- Support BRF Ministries with a regular donation;
- Support us with a one-off gift;
- Consider leaving a gift to BRF Ministries in your will (see page 157);
- Encourage your church to support BRF Ministries as part of your church's giving to home mission – perhaps focusing on a specific ministry;
- Most important of all, support BRF Ministries with your prayers.

Donate at **brf.org.uk/donate** or use the form on pages 137–38.

A friend indeed

I no longer call you servants, because a servant does not know his master's business. Instead, I have called you friends, for everything that I learned from my Father I have made known to you. You did not choose me, but I chose you and appointed you so that you might go and bear fruit – fruit that will last – and so that whatever you ask in my name the Father will give you.

JOHN 15:15–16 (NIV)

In this verse Jesus is speaking to his disciples in the upper room, a farewell and a sending out, words of comfort and empowerment to get them through the coming days. Here he makes it explicit, those gathered in the room are his friends. Their relationship has transcended that of master and servant through the sharing of knowledge. For a servant simply follows the orders of the master while a friend with profound understanding can take initiative and carry ideas forward – and ultimately bear lasting fruit.

For over 100 years, BRF Ministries has been working to share the knowledge of the gospel with as many people of all ages as possible – from BRF Resources, such as our *Guidelines* Bible reading notes, to the work of our other ministries: Anna Chaplaincy, Messy Church, and Parenting for Faith. It is our goal not only to share the Bible but to give people the tools for deeper understanding and for building a friendship with God that they can then take forward and, in their own lives and communities, bear fruit.

Our work is made possible through kind donations from individuals, charitable trusts and gifts in wills. If you would like to support our work you can become a Friend of BRF Ministries by making a monthly gift of £2 or more – we thank you for your friendship.

Find out more at **brf.org.uk/donate** or get in touch with us on **01865 319700** or via **giving@brf.org.uk**.

We thank you for your support and your prayers.

The fundraising team at BRF Ministries

Give. Pray. Get involved.
brf.org.uk

GUIDELINES SUBSCRIPTION RATES

Please note our new subscription rates, current until 30 April 2027:

Individual subscriptions
covering three issues for under six copies, payable in advance (including postage & packing):

	UK	Europe	Rest of world
Guidelines 1-year subscription	£25.20	£37.50	£44.25

Copies may also be obtained from Christian bookshops:

Guidelines	£5.99 per copy

All our Bible reading notes can be ordered online by visiting **brfresources.org.uk/subscriptions**

GUIDELINES SUBSCRIPTION FORM

To set up a recurring subscription, please go to
brfresources.org.uk/subscriptions

Title .... First name/initials .... Surname ....

Address ....

.... Postcode ....

Telephone .... Email ....

Please send ***Guidelines*** beginning with the September 2026 / January 2027 / May 2027 issue (*delete as appropriate*):

(*please tick box*)	**UK**	**Europe**	**Rest of world**
Guidelines 1-year subscription	☐ £25.20	☐ £37.50	☐ £44.25

Optional donation to support the work of BRF Ministries £ ....

Total enclosed £ .... (cheques should be made payable to 'BRF')

Please complete and return the Gift Aid declaration on page 138 to make your donation even more valuable to us.

Please charge my MasterCard / Visa with £ ....

Card no. ☐☐☐☐ ☐☐☐☐ ☐☐☐☐ ☐☐☐☐

Expires end ☐☐ (M M) ☐☐ (Y Y)

We will use your personal data to process this order. From time to time we may send you information about the work of BRF Ministries. Please contact us if you wish to discuss your mailing preferences **brf.org.uk/privacy**

Please return this form with the appropriate payment to:
BRF Ministries, 15 The Chambers, Vineyard, Abingdon OX14 3FE
For terms and cancellation information, please visit **brfresources.org.uk/terms**.